J. Dyer Ball

Cantonese made Easy

Salzwasser

J. Dyer Ball

Cantonese made Easy

1. Auflage | ISBN: 978-3-84604-798-9

Erscheinungsort: Frankfurt, Deutschland

Erscheinungsjahr: 2020

Salzwasser Verlag GmbH

Reprint of the original, first published in 1904.

CANTONESE MADE EASY:

A BOOK OF SIMPLE SENTENCES IN THE CANTONESE DIALECT, WITH
FREE AND LITERAL TRANSLATIONS, AND DIRECTIONS
FOR THE RENDERING OF ENGLISH GRAM-
MATICAL FORMS IN CHINESE.

THIRD EDITION.
REVISED AND ENLARGED.

BY

J. DYER BALL, M.R.A.S., ETC.,

OF HER MAJESTY'S CIVIL SERVICE, HONGKONG.

Author of 'Easy Sentences in the Hakka Dialect with a Vocabulary,' 'How to Speak
Cantonese,' 'The Cantonese-made-Easy Vocabulary,' 'Readings in Cantonese
Colloquial,' 'An English-Cantonese Pocket Vocabulary without
the Chinese Characters or Tonic Marks,' 'Hakka
Made Easy,' and 'Things Chinese.'

Singapore:

KELLY & WALSH, LIMITED, PRINTERS.

1904.

CONTENTS.

PREFACES.

PREFACE

TO THE FIRST EDITION.

THIS little book is meant to supply a want. The Author has heard a beginner in Chinese sadly lamenting the difficulty he had in the use of his phrase-book to know what the Chinese words really meant. Before him and before many a learner, there appear on the opened pages of his book sentences in English and sentences in Chinese. He reads the English and his Chinese teacher reads the Chinese over to him until he learns the sounds. By dint of memory he learns that a certain English sentence is expressed in Chinese by certain Chinese words, which he supposes are the equivalents of the English words; but as soon as he commences to analyse the two sentences—to place them side by side, he finds that there seems to be very little similarity between the two. The one often has more words by far than the other; there are no numbers, no moods, no tenses, or but halting expedients to represent them, which are well nigh unintelligible to him; and the use of his dictionary, at first, affords him but little assistance in his attempts to pick asunder the component parts of a Chinese sentence, for either he does not find the word that is given in his phrase-book, or he is embarrassed by the multiplicity of renderings for one word.

Arrangement of this Book.

In some of the first books in Cantonese and English by the veteran sinologists, this difficulty was in a great measure met by a literal as well as a free translation being given of the Chinese. The Author has resuscitated this old plan and trusts it will be found of service. In some cases it will be found, however, that it has been well nigh impossible, on account of the idiomatic differences of the two languages, to give a perfectly intelligible and literal rendering of the Chinese; for it sometimes happens, as GEORGE MACDONALD well remarks, that:—'It is often curious how a literal rendering, 'even when it gives quite the meaning, will not do, because of the different

'ranks of the two words in their respective languages.' *(Adela Cathcart*, p. 34.)
Yet, with the object of pointing out the connection of the different words
and their respective places in the sentence, even a poor literal translation
will assist the learner far better to grasp the construction of the sentence and
the real meaning of the words than a free translation, which must necessarily
often be but a paraphrase of the Chinese.

When two or more English words represent one Chinese word, the
Author has, in the literal translation, connected them by a hyphen, and the
same holds good of the Chinese and English.   Any exceptions to this are so
plain that there is no necessity to make any note of them.

The fault of most phrase-books in Chinese is the multiplying Chinese
words in a sentence ; especially do such books delight in a redundancy of
particles ; one is almost sickened by a glance through some of the phrase-books
in use where ʿko koʾ, ₒni koʾ, keʾ, and many other particles are brought in at
any time and every time to the detriment of the learner's fluency in speaking.
The consequence of this fault is that learners pile up the component parts of
a sentence until the outcome is something wonderful to hearken to, and more
like a foreign language than good Chinese.   The Chinese are fonder of
expressing themselves in a terse and concise manner than most book-makers
represent them as doing.   Redundant words are cut out of good Chinese
colloquial with an unsparing hand : and it would be a good thing for a learner
to lay it down as a general rule that if it is possible to express his meaning
with few words, he should do so ; for though to his own ear the addition of
words may make the meaning plainer, it has probably a directly contrary
effect on a Chinese ear.

Compare :—

ʿNéí ₂laí tòʾ ₒni shüʾ k'ap₂ ʿpéí ʿko koʾ ₂shü kwoʾ ʿngo ʿt'aí kínʾ ₂lá.
and

₂Laí ₒni shüʾ ʿpéí ʿko pò² ₂shü ʿngo ʿt'aí.

There is often also no distinction made in phrase books between the
colloquial and book language : immediately after a sentence which would be
understood by any woman or child comes one so bookish that if the learner
were to attempt to air his newly-acquired knowledge, thus obtained, out of
the range of his study or of the ears of his erudite teacher, he would find his
talk utterly unintelligible to the mass of his hearers.   In short, a hotchpotch
of anything and everything is thrown together, mixed and pure, Cantonese
and provincialisms, and the result is a phrase-book.

Many of the simplest and commonest forms of expression are entirely
omitted even in books of considerable size where want of space could be no
excuse.

There is often also apparent in these books an evident attempt to *put* the English sentence, which the compiler chooses, into Chinese, ignoring often to a great extent the simple fact that the idiom is essentially English; and the result is a sentence composed of Chinese words, which is either constructed on an English idiom wholly foreign to the genius of the language, or stilted in order to convey the whole meaning of the English sentence into Chinese; or else the two sentences are not the counterparts of each other, and the learner is misled.

Knowing these defects, the Author has endeavoured to avoid them.

It appeared to him that a compiler should endeavour above everything else to have his Chinese perfect and readable, or *shun*, as a Chinese would term it, and then try his best to render the Chinese into English. Under such conditions there is more likelihood of getting good Chinese into our phrase-books than when the opposite plan is tried.

Daily intercourse for nearly a quarter of a century with all classes of Chinese in their daily life, and years of daily contact with all grades of Chinese in the course of his official duties, where no attempts, or but few, are made to adapt themselves to the foreign ear, have placed him, he believes, in an exceptionally favourable position to hear and note the different idioms of good Cantonese. He has endeavoured to embody a number of them in this book, which, if it meets with a favourable reception, might induce him to attempt something more pretentious on a future occasion.

Nothing, he hopes, will be found amongst the fifteen Lessons but pure good colloquial; and from the examples given in that part of the book, as well as in the part which follows, the learner will be able to frame other sentences.

In learning Cantonese the learner should aim first at acquiring such common idioms and such words as to make himself understood by even the illiterate class, for then all classes will understand him. Starting in this manner he will lay a good solid foundation for his colloquial, which will stand him in good stead all through his stay in China. After this foundation is laid he can easily acquire the mixed colloquial, composed principally of what he has already learned, and partly of book terms; and if he has previously pleased the illiterate ear, qualify himself to please the fastidious taste of the scholar. Though there is no hard and fast line between these two forms of colloquial, as they merge more or less into each other, there is still a distinction. And the learner should keep this distinction in his mind and ask his teacher whether any new phrase he comes across is colloquial or not. Without this precaution he will find himself talking in a most ridiculous style, at one breath, as it were, using Johnsonian words and pure English.

In most, if not all, phrase-books the tones seem to be a thing of secondary importance. If the compiler carefully gives the tones, as he finds them in his dictionary, he congratulates himself on at least stretching a point. As a general rule, no attempt is ever made to give the tones as they are spoken, or, when the attempt has been made, the compiler has had so little idea of the frequency of difference between colloquial and book tones that his attempts to point one or two out have not been of the practical use they might have been. It is one thing to read a book and utter all the tones correctly, but quite another thing to explain to a Chinese the contents of a few pages thereof, and if the speaker sticks to the same tones in speaking as in reading he will not find all he says is understood. It is, the Author believes, an ignoring of this fact that often spoils foreigners' Chinese. The awkward thing about ignoring these tones in books, for the use of those who wish to learn to speak Chinese, is that the learner attempts to say the word in the tone that he sees it marked in his book or dictionary, the consequence being that he systematically mispronounces it, while if the tone were marked properly, he would at least attempt to pronounce it properly.

The colloquial tones in this book are given instead of those used in the book language.

It will be noticed that occasionally the tones of one word are different in different connections.

Learners may at once make up their minds to the belief that there are more tones in the Chinese than many of the old scholars will give credit for. The *chung yap* is introduced in this phrase book. The man who pretends to doubt its existence may as well confess at once that he knows nothing about differences in tones ; it was well known by one or two of the older sinologists in olden times, but was well-nigh forgotten until unearthed recently. There, perhaps, is more excuse for the scepticism that exists about some of the other tones, though there can be no doubt as to their existence.

Instead, then, of only eight tones in Cantonese, it is the fact that there are sixteen well-defined tones at least, and possibly one or two others as well, affecting only a very few words. This last need not, however, trouble the learner at first. It is well that he should know at the same time that he must not attempt to fit every Chinese word into the only tone, perchance, assigned to it by the dictionaries. Cantonese will not be confined in that way, and much of the poor pronunciation of Chinese in the past by Europeans is on account of their persistent attempts to pronounce all Chinese words as if they must belong to one or other of the eight or nine tones their dictionaries told them about. Get a good teacher, then copy him exactly, no matter what your dictionary may say about the tone of the word ; for it is important that the beginner, who wishes to do more than just run a chance of being partially understood, should pay particular attention to these important tones, though at the same time let him not run into the other extreme of hesitating before he utters a word to think what tone it should be in. If he can manage to get fluent in Chinese idioms, an occasional mistake in the tones is not of such vital importance, though to be deprecated.

Grammar.

The Directions for rendering English Grammatical Forms and Idioms into Chinese and *vice versâ* will, it is hoped, prove of service in enabling the beginner to form a conception of the mode in which English grammatical forms may be rendered in Chinese, a language which at first sight appears to be devoid of all grammar. The construction of the component parts and the building up of the sentence from its component phrases will also appear to a certain extent.

The notes are not exhaustive, but it is hoped that they are of sufficient variety and length to give the learner such an idea of the construction of the colloquial, and of many of its idioms, as to enable him to avoid egregious errors.

So little has been attempted in this way hitherto, that it is with considerable diffidence one makes the attempt to lay down instructions, when hitherto the learner has generally had to bungle on as well as he could himself.

It is hoped, however, that the experience of one who has made the study of Chinese a life-work will not prove useless to the beginner.

The study of Chinese is sufficiently difficult to make every little hint a desideratum.

Final Particles.

The Final Particles are most useful little words, quite altering the whole force of the sentence when differently applied. These little particles at the end of a sentence are often put to a dreadful martyrdom in beginners' books. The student must not suppose that, because they are so plentifully sprinkled over the pages of his book, he cannot close his mouth without enunciating one or two of them, as he would punctuate each of his written sentences. They are, in fact, often left out, with advantage ; but when left out, to make up for their absence, the voice lingers often on the last word in the sentence longer than it would otherwise do, and with a peculiar intonation and rising inflection, going, in fact, into a Rising Tone. At other times it goes into the variant of the Upper Even Tone, the tone taking often the place of the final, though at the same time these tones are often used with finals as well.

Too little attention has been paid to them hitherto. Our dictionaries do not contain all that are in use. A list appears of as many as the compiler has been able to discover up to the present time with their tonal variations; but it is not at all improbable that there are more to be discovered. Nearly half of this list is not to be found in the dictionaries. If the finals used in the different dialects and sub-dialects of Cantonese were included, the list might be made of an enormous length, as, for instance, in the Shun-tak dialect, to mention a few instances amongst many, we have the finals, *téi, tí,* and others, besides those in use in pure Cantonese.

This is, however, not the place to go into a dissertation on the finals, but the hint may be of use if taken advantage of, for there are a great many more shades of meaning to be expressed by a proper use of these little words than most Europeans have ever dreamt of.

Chinese Characters.

The Chinese characters are given more as a guide to the teacher than for use by the beginner. If the latter can and will take advice it is this :—Don't trouble yourself with the character, or the book language at first. If you will learn the characters, learn them out of the colloquial books for the first year, and then, when you are tolerably proficient in colloquial, a knowledge of the book way of expressing what you have already acquired in colloquial will not be apt to confuse you, or spoil your colloquial.

One thing at a time is enough. If you wish to speak Chinese well, learn to speak it before you learn to read it. A Chinese child learns to speak his native tongue before he learns to read it ; and yet we, go-ahead Westerners, think we know better than Dame Nature, and insist on learning two languages (the book language and the colloquial) at the same time—two languages which, be it remembered, are so alike and yet so dissimilar as to create no end of a confusion in the tyro's brain. The result is that we produce but few good speakers of Chinese.

Above all things let him who would speak Chinese not be ashamed to talk whenever he has a chance. Air his Chinese at all times : it will get musty if he does not. What does it matter if he does make mistakes at first ? If he finds he is not understood when he puts a thing in one way, then let him put it in another. He should try to get up a pretty extensive vocabulary of apparent synonyms, and by experience and experiment he will learn what words are best understood by different classes of people, and what are the right words to use. Of course all this implies a great deal of patience ; but if a man has no patience, he had better not come to Far Cathay.

Orthography.

The orthography is WILLIAMS's with the exception of some slight variations where necessary.

The classes of variants are given below, so that the scholar may find no difficulty in using WILLIAMS's Tonic Dictionary or EITEL's Chinese Dictionary.

In this book.	In Williams' and Eitel's.
éí	í (or i in Eitel's.)
ŏ	éu
ŏû	ui
wú	ú
wúí	ui
yí	í (or i in Eitel's.)
yû	û

If the beginner would be a good speaker, let him not follow the pronunciations given in Dictionaries if he finds such to clash with that of his teacher, provided he has a good one, but imitate the latter. Let him remember :—

1st. That the dictionaries have been made by Europeans to whom Chinese was not a native tongue, and that consequently they are not free from errors.

2nd. Also let him remember that at the best it is but a halting expedient to attempt to represent Chinese sounds by the letters of an alphabet, which, as we are accustomed to use them in our own language, are never in every case capable of producing the identical Chinese sound.

3rd. Let him also remember that some of the Chinese assistants that Dictionary makers have depended on for their pronunciations, were not pure Cantonese speakers.

These several reasons will be sufficient to assure him of the necessity for adhering to the above advice ; and when he becomes a proficient in the use of this beautiful (when spoken in its purity) language, he will see an additional reason in the miserable pronunciation of some Europeans, who have considered their dictionaries wiser than the Chinese themselves ; and he may be gratified by being told by the Chinese that his pronunciation is clearer and better in many respects than many a native's.

In conclusion, the author may express the hope—a hope that has actuated him throughout the preparation, that this little book will prove a help in the study of a tongue which he has known and spoken from his earliest infancy. Should it prove of assistance to those who, unlike him, have not been able to avail themselves of the easiest and best mode of learning it, he will be proud that these efforts have proved capable of assisting those who desire to acquire a knowledge of this, one of the finest and oldest languages in China.

His thanks are due to Mr. H. A. GILES of H. M.'s Consular Service for again permitting him to make use of his arrangement of sentences and the plan of his book, as far as the first part of it is concerned, which it will be seen he has considerably enlarged upon.

Mr. A. FALCONER, of the Government Central School, Hongkong, has also kindly assisted him in correcting proof sheets.

＊   ＊   ＊   ＊   ＊   ＊   ＊   ＊

After having written out the whole of the lessons, and while they were in the press, the compiler's attention was called to Mr. PARKER's orthography as applied to the Cantonese: and finding that in one instance it supplied a want that he had felt, and that in another instance it represented a sound which had not been brought out clearly, his spelling in both these instances was modified in conformity with Mr. PARKER's system. He cannot endorse Mr. PARKER's attempts in their entirety (his attempts to rid the orthography from diacritical marks do not always appear to be the best); especially all the conclusions he arrives at as exemplified by his orthography, that is to say, if he understands what the spelling always refers to, but unfortunately his syllabary is printed without any Chinese characters, so that one scarcely knows what word the new combination of letters always represents. Finding that in certain cases Mr. PARKER's was an improvement on the current orthography, other cases have also been referred to Mr. PARKER's syllabary, and the author must acknowledge occasional assistance he has derived from such a reference while working by the guidance of his ear to free himself from the, in too many cases, barbarous and incorrect spellings used by the dictionaries. He has been pleased to find, on reference to Mr. PARKER's syllabary, that he also had arrived in the majority of instances at the same conclusions that the author had. This, he trusts, will give more confidence in the accuracy of those sounds represented by Mr. PARKER and himself to those who may be inclined to look with suspicion upon and doubt the propriety of any change, however simple, in the admirable adaptation of Sir WILLIAM JONES's system of spelling made in his younger days by that venerable and learned sinologist, Dr. WILLIAMS.

J. DYER BALL.

HONGKONG, 1883.

———

PREFACE

TO THE SECOND EDITION.

♦

IT is now rather more than four years since the first edition, of five hundred copies, of this book was published. Uncertain of the success of the venture at the time the pamphlet was but limited in its scope. The disposal of the first edition and the approval the book has met with has led the author to issue a second edition of the same work, which, though running on the same lines as the first edition, has been considerably enlarged. The first part, that containing the fifteen lessons, may at first sight appear to be the same in the two editions, but though the same number of pages are occupied, it will be found that there are many more sentences in this part of the book than formerly. Great care has also been exercised in a careful revision of the lessons, and here the author must acknowledge the great assistance rendered to him by the Hon. J. H. STEWART LOCKHART, C.M.G., who kindly volunteered to assist him.

In the second, or Grammatical portion, it will be seen that thirty-six pages are added. A new table of the Classifiers has been drawn up, from which it has been attempted to exclude words not rightly entitled to the name of Classifiers, though often so called, and these words have been placed in a list by themselves. A better table of the Personal Pronouns has also been prepared. An important addition has likewise been the lists of the idiomatic uses of verbs, and other additions, it will be seen, have been made, all of which the author trusts will make the book more useful. The old matter has also been revised.

A new feature appears in the shape of an Index to the Second part, which will no doubt render reference to passages sought for easier than with the help of the table of contents alone, which is still retained. In the Introduction the tones have been more fully treated.

It has been the author's endeavour in what may be called the Grammatical portion of the book not so much to lay down Grammatical Rules describing the structure of the language irrespective of its analogy to other languages; but it has been his aim so to word these rules as to show the learner the difference between his native language and that he is endeavouring to acquire, for in detecting the points of resemblance and difference between his own language and one foreign to him will he be the better able to appreciate the similarity and dissimilarity between the two languages. It is but a waste of time to draw up a Chinese Grammar on the same lines as an English Grammar; such Grammars are useful to those who wish to learn the structure of their own language, but to those who already know something of the Grammar of one language this knowledge is best utilised by being used as a vantage ground. The knowledge already acquired is compared with what it is desired to acquire. The mind instead of being burdened with going over old ground has its powers left free to tabulate the new knowledge under the two heads of 'the same as I learnt before, I do not need to trouble about that,' and the other head of 'this is different from what I learnt before, I must try and remember this.'

Any learner who desires to acquire a new language, if he wishes to make any progress, must consciously or unconsciously thus tabulate his knowledge. If it is not already done for him in the books he uses, his time is taken up with wading through a mass of rules and examples to pick out what is new to him. His time is saved and the acquisition of the language rendered easier if it is done beforehand for him.

Exception has been taken by one or two to the use of the literal translation of the Chinese into English on account of its barbarous nature, but its manifest advantages to the beginner are so obvious, not only theoretically but in actual practice in the use of this book, that the author's predilections in its favour are confirmed. As to its being barbarous, what does barbarous mean? Simply that anything is outside of our pale of civilization and customary mode of expression, etc. A literal translation of any language into English proves more or less barbarous: this is even true with regard to the classic languages of ancient Greece and Rome.

As a hint to the use this literal translation may be put, the following passage is given from an essay by PROCTOR with regard to the use of literal translations, such as the Hamiltonian method is based on, the literal translation employed by the author of the present work being very like those. Mr. PROCTOR says :—' Take then first * * a passage * * and go carefully over it, word for word as it stands. * * * Next, read it over several words at a time. After this, read the English through alone, and then turn to the original, and read that through. You will find that by this time you can read the original understandingly. Take the passage next * * and turn it into English by a free translation—not too free, but just free enough to be good English. Now follows what in practice I found the most improving part of the whole work. Make a word-for-word translation in the exact order of the words in the original, and note what this tells you of the character of the idiom and also of the mental peculiarities of the nation who * * own the language you are dealing with. ' (*Miscellaneous Essays*, by R. A. PROCTER.)

J. DYER BALL.

HONGKONG, 1887.

PREFACE

TO THE THIRD EDITION.

A NUMBER of years has now passed since the second edition of a thousand copies of this book was published, and it has been out of print for some time. The author regrets the long delay and the impossibility of providing the numerous students with this *vade mecum* before now.

Some additions, it will be noticed, have been made to this edition. Attention has been most fully called to those most important tones—the variants, which form a part of the very language itself; and whose very existence has been most grudgingly acknowledged by foreigners—the cachet of recognition being still largely denied them, and yet it is impossible to speak Chinese (Cantonese) correctly without constantly using them. A book might be written on their uses and occurrences.

It being so absolutely necessary to employ the correct titles and forms of address when speaking to natives of different status, or when speaking of one's own countrymen of different social standing, a list of forms of addresses, used in conversation with the persons themselves, whether relatives or strangers, and modes of mentioning them when talking about them, is one of the new features in the present edition. It must tend to a still further lowering of the Chinese idea of the 'outside barbarian' to hear his fellow-countryman style one of their own officials simply *sin sháng*, when he is entitled from his position to be spoken of as *lò ye*, *tái lò ye*, or *tái yan*, to say nothing of the disuse of respectful terms for relatives.

Another list is that of words of the higgledy-piggledy order, very commonly used, but very few of which appear in our dictionaries of the Chinese language.

It is hoped that these and other additions and alterations will tend to make the book even more useful in the future than it has been in the past.

J. DYER BALL.

HONGKONG, 1902.

INTRODUCTION.

THE CANTONESE DIALECT OR LANGUAGE.

An impression appears to have got abroad that Mandarin is the language of China, and that Cantonese and the other languages spoken in China are but dialects of it. The impression is an erroneous one. One might as well say that Spanish was the language of the Iberian Peninsula and that Portuguese, as well as the other Romanic languages spoken elsewhere, were dialects of it. There is no doubt that, as with Spanish in the Peninsula, Mandarin in some one or other of its various dialects is the language of a large portion of China (say of thirteen out of the eighteen provinces), but no less is Cantonese in some one or other of *its* numerous dialects the language of a great many of the inhabitants of the two provinces of Kwangtung and Kwangsi, (which two provinces have a population roughly stated to be equal to that of England). It is true that the Mandarin is used as a *lingua franca* in all official courts and Government offices throughout the whole of China ; but though more than five hundred years ago, for a considerable time in English history, French was the Court language of England, yet there was an English language, though it may have been despised by those who knew nothing but French.

One of the unfortunate things about terming these different languages in China dialects, is to lead those who know nothing of the subject to suppose that Cantonese is merely a local *patois* differentiated from the Mandarin by dialectic peculiarities, and that those who speak it differ as far from what is generally supposed to be a correct method of speaking their native tongue, as a Somerset man or Yorkshireman who speaks his native dialect does from an educated Englishman, who, by virtue of his education and culture, has sunk all the peculiarities of pronunciation which inevitably point out the illiterate countryman.

In fact, the Cantonese is more nearly akin to the ancient language of China, spoken about 3,000 years ago, than the speech of other parts of China. It is more ancient itself than the other so-called dialects of China, and to prevent any false ideas of its importance the following extract is given from the Preface to Douglas' Dictionary of the Amoy language, the statements in which are equally applicable to Cantonese. It is as follows, viz.:—

'But such words as "Dialect" or "Colloquial" give an erroneous conception of its nature. It is not a mere colloquial dialect or patois; it is spoken by the highest ranks just as by the common people, by the most learned just as by the most ignorant; learned men indeed add a few polite or pedantic phrases, but these are mere excrescences, (and even they are pronounced' according to the Cantonese sounds), 'while the main body and staple of the spoken language of the most refined and learned classes is the same as that of coolies, labourers, and boatmen.

'Nor does the term "dialect" convey anything like a correct idea of its distinctive character; it is no mere dialectic variety of some other language; it is a distinct language, one of the many and widely differing languages which divide among them the soil of China. * * *

'A very considerable number of the spoken languages of China have been already more or less studied by European and American residents in the country, such as the Mandarin, the Hakka, the vernaculars of Canton and Amoy, and several others. These are not dialects of one language; they are cognate languages, bearing to each other a relation similar to that which subsists between the Arabic, the Hebrew, the Syriac, the Ethiopic, and the other members of the Semitic family; or, again, between English, German, Dutch, Danish, Swedish, etc.

'There is another serious objection to the use of the term "dialect" as applied to these languages, namely, that within each of them there exist *real dialects*. For instance, the Mandarin contains within itself three very marked "dialects," the Northern, spoken at Peking; the Southern, spoken at Nanking and Soochow; and the Western, spoken in the Provinces of Szechuen, Hoopeh, etc.'

It may be stated that it is as absurd for any one who intends to reside in Hongkong, Canton, or Macao, and who wishes to learn Chinese to take up the study of Mandarin, as it would be for a German, who was about to settle in London, to learn French in order to be able to converse with the English.

Cantonese has its 'real dialects,' some of which are spoken by tens of thousands, or hundreds of thousands of natives, and which if they were spoken by the inhabitants of some insignificant group of islands in the Pacific with only a tithe of the population would be honoured by the name of languages. These 'subordinate dialects' of the Cantonese are again subdivided into many little divisions spoken in different cities or towns, or groups of cities, towns, and villages where peculiar colloquialisms prevail. Some of these dialects of Cantonese are as follows, viz. :—

The San Wíú	The Hŏng Shan	The Fá Yün	The Shíú Hing
., San Ning	,. Shun Tak	,. Ts'ing Yün	., Yŏng Kong
,, Yan P'ing	,. Há Pún Yü	., Sám Shŏü	,, Lín Chaú
., Hoí P'ing	,. Tung Kwún	,, Ts'ung Fá	,, Shíú Kwán
., Hok Shán	,, Waí Chaú	,, Shŏng Pún Yü	,, Ying Tak

Besides these there are the dialects in the Há Sz Fú, The Lower Four Prefectures of the Province.

———

The correct pronunciation of pure Cantonese.

So far is this minute sub-division carried that even in the city of Canton itself, the seat and centre of pure Cantonese, more than one pronunciation of words is used ; the standard, however, being the Saí Kwán wá, or West End speech, to which the learner should endeavour to assimilate his talk. It has been the author's endeavour to give this pronunciation, or, at all events, the Cantonese, and the students of this book may take it as a fact that it is Cantonese, and pure Cantonese, that is given ; and that where the author has corrected the orthography of WILLIAMS and EITEL it is because this orthography in such cases does not represent pure Cantonese, such, for instance, as in the spelling of the whole series of words 女 *nöü*, 去 *höü*, etc., which these authors give most unfortunately as *nü*, *hü*, etc., such sounds being abominable Cantonese—not pure Cantonese at all, but Saí Chíú Dialect or some other wretched dialect, notwithstanding they have the sanction of such sinologues as WILLIAMS, EITEL, and CHALMERS. Those who know Chinese thoroughly will know that the author is throwing no slur on the masterly scholarship displayed by these men when he says that their pronunciation of Cantonese, as shewn by their orthography, in many instances is neither pure nor correct.

It is a great pity that Dr. EITEL, in his new Dictionary, has not followed the lead of good speakers of pure Cantonese instead of perpetuating the mistakes of Dr. WILLIAMS—mistakes due partly to the implicit following of a Chinese author's ideas of pronunciation, and mistakes more excusable in the olden days than at the present time.

To those who are inclined to be suspicious of any change in an established orthography of Chinese by Europeans, the fact that the author is not alone in this changing of the mode of representing another class of sounds may give more confidence to their acceptance of it, and to those who know Mr. PARKER's wonderfully acute ear for Chinese sounds the following extracts may help to confirm their acceptance of such changes.

'The only place where a really short *e* comes in, * * is in the diphthong *ei* (as in feint * *). This sound is * * actually ignored by WILLIAMS in favour of *i*, as in the English *thee*, a Cantonese sound which only exists in one or two colloquial words such as *mi, ni,* etc.' *China Review*, Vol. 8, p. 364.

And again, ' but, unfortunately WILLIAMS uses *i* to represent both the *ee* and *ei* as in feel and feint.' *China Review*, Vol. 8, p. 365.

He again says in a paper on 'the Comparative study of Chinese dialects,' published in the transactions of the North China Branch of the Royal Asiatic Society: 'In Dr. WILLIAMS' dictionary again, several classes of vowels existing in theory, according to the standard *in nubibus*, encumber the work, when one vowel would have stood in each case for them all. One of the nine regular tones, too, is entirely ignored ; and the whole class of colloquial tones called the *pín yam*, which form so striking an element of quasi-inflection in the pure Cantonese dialect, has been completely overlooked. Dr. EITEL, in his corrected edition of the same Dictionary, has introduced the ninth regular tone, but he likewise, instead of adhering steadfastly (as did Mr. WADE in the case of the Metropolitan Pekingese), to the Metropolitan Cantonese, has, by overlooking these colloquial tones, once more lost the opportunity of firmly establishing another standard dialect.'

The opinion of another enthusiastic student of Cantonese, than whom it is difficult to find one showing greater zeal in all matters connected with the language, (the author refers to The Hon. J. H. STEWART-LOCKHART, C.M.G.), likewise says :—' It is much to be regretted that Dr. EITEL'S . . Dictionary, though excellent in many ways, has not modified the spelling in WILLIAMS'.' *China Review*, Vol. X., p. 312.

The matter resolves itself into simply this, whether we are to go on perpetrating mistakes by accepting the orthography of WILLIAMS and EITEL *in extenso*—in every minute particular, when it is a well-known fact by those who speak pure Cantonese that this orthography in all its particulars is not pure Cantonese by a long way, but is mixed up with local pronunciations, or whether we are to try to get an English transliteration of Chinese sounds, which shall attempt to approach as near as possible to the standard Cantonese, that spoken in the city of Canton itself. That such attempts may be open to partial failures in some particulars none knows better than the author himself, but because the matter is a difficult one to tackle there is no reason why we should go on in the old ruts. They are getting rather worn out now after half a century of use and it is time that better ways were followed.

A curious argument is sometimes used as a reason for not conforming to a standard—a real standard and a pure one—namely, that it does not much matter as long as they, the Europeans or Americans, who speak Chinese are understood. In this argument it is taken for granted that they must be understood, but they are often not.

A good story is told of an Englishman in Russia coming across a Russian, who accosted him in broad Yorkshire to the astonishment of the Briton, the Russian being under the impression that he was conversing in good English, he having availed himself of the services of an Englishman to learn his, the Englishman's, native language, but unfortunately the teacher spoke a dialect, Yorkshire, which is not now considered pure English.

This is bad enough, but supposing the Russian, instead of learning from an Englishman, had used books to acquire the language, and that these books had taught him to invariably leave off the initial *h*, as cockneys do ; to pronounce the *s*, as if it were a *z*, in imitation of the Somerset dialect ; to pronounce the article *the*, as if it were a *t* alone, in imitation of Yorkshire ; and to pronounce every word like *bay, day, fay, gay, hay, jay, lay, may, nay, pay, ray, say, way*, as if they were spelled *be, de, fee, gee, he, ge, lea, me, knee, pea, re, see, we*, and other mispronunciations of the same character. What a delightful hotch-potch this would be ! This then may give an idea of what results ensue in Chinese from the orthography of some of the books that are now in use by Europeans for learning Chinese.

What would be thought of an argument to the effect that it mattered little to the Russian, as many English dropped their *h* all through the length and breadth of the land, that likewise numbers of genuine Englishmen pronounced the *the* as *t* alone, and that there were not a few that pronounced the *s* as a *z*, and that the other mispronunciations were also in use in English ?

And yet the same style of argument is used with regard to these dialectic pronunciations of Cantonese by some book makers.

The following statement by Mr. PARKER is conclusive on the point, except to those who are prejudiced against any conclusion except their own :—' The argument so frequently used that, in the presence of so many conflicting forms of Cantonese it is unwise to make a special study of one, ought to condemn itself without demonstration to every logical student, apart from the obvious fact that the dialect of a metropolis, as spoken by the most highly educated classes, is *primâ facie* more likely to be a standard and to be more widely known than a dialect spoken by less educated persons in the country, or in a town less thickly populated than the metropolis.'—*China Review*, Vol. 8, p. 367.

THE TONES.

Regarding the Tones one writer says, 'It is not true that the tones are an attribute belonging to monosyllabic and isolating languages only. Every language may be said to have certain tones, recurring under certain conditions; only they are more pronounced in some languages than in others, and they are undefined and fluctuating until science gets hold of them and they are codified. The accents of the Vedas, it appears, like the Greek accents, were real tones in the Chinese sense, that is to say they marked not only the stress of the voice, but also its pitch and inflection, and in our modern European languages, when attention is paid to correct pronunciation as in works on elocution, the rise and fall of the voice is carefully indicated.

' In their inception the tones must, I think, be viewed as a physiological phenomenon; in their progress they are conventional, and may in the end become rigid. Languages with a fully developed system of agglutination or inflection, capable of expressing the various relations of logical synthesis, may employ them for psychological purposes, to indicate yet finer shades of meaning or subjective modes not otherwise provided for in the language. In languages of a lower type, which eschew the use of an elaborate formal apparatus or are in advanced stage of detrition, they may serve to do duty as functional marks, either as the result of a spontaneous differentiation or in consequence of the loss of derivative particles. In any case the accent will be the more marked and developed, the poorer the stock of phonetic elements, the feebler the power of composition and derivation, and the more primitive the grammatical structure. And these conditions are fulfilled in the highest degree in the monosyllabic languages.

' With their codification the tones enter upon a new phase of existence. What was first a habit of the individual, or the custom of a community, is now invested with the authority of a law. A new and highly artificial moment begins to operate, and operates the more surely, the greater and the more universal the influence of letters upon society. Its tendency is conservative; its effect to retard further development which it cannot altogether arrest. The system may from time to time adjust itself to the exigencies of the living tongue, but, as a rule, a wide gulf will separate the popular idiom from the language of literature; and this applies as well to the articulation and manner of intonation as to idiomatic peculiarities.'— (A. VON ROSTHORN, Ph. D. in *China Review*, Vol. XXII, p. 448.)

The Chinese utter the words in the right tone, but the majority of them do not know anything about tones, more than possessing the ability without being aware of the name of the tones, to pronounce them correctly, just as in English we would give the right emphasis and the right accent to the words in a sentence.

When the native scholars awoke to the idea of the tones and discovered that they, as well as all their countrymen and ancestors, had been using tones all their lives and every time they opened their mouths to speak, they naturally wished to find out the origin of their use. The Shí King, 'The Book of Odes,' one of the Chinese Classics, which book contains 'as in a mirror, the circumstances, the thoughts, the habits, the joys and sorrows of persons of all classes of society in China 3,000 years ago,' affords by its rhymes the means of studying the tones in the earliest period of Chinese history. Dr. A. von Rosthorn says regarding this: ' A great deal has ' been written on the rhymes of the Shih by native authors, and the evidence ' which has been brought to bear upon the subject seems to favour the ' assumption that the tones existed even in the earliest known specimens of ' the language, but that they were used unconsciously and with a considerable ' degree of latitude.' ' The conscious discrimination of the tones and their ' codification were not arrived at until the latter part of the 5th Century, ' A. D. Chou Yu and Shên Yo are the names usually associated with ' their discovery; but it is more probable that they were first observed by ' the Indian missionaries,' to whom ' the tones were not an altogether new ' phenomenon ＊ ＊ ＊ for they had already studied the accents and quantities ' in the language of the Vedas, and these were the elements out of which ' the Chinese tones undoubtedly grew.' As Dr. Edkins says, ' accustomed to ' the unrivalled accuracy in phonetic analysis of the Sanscrit alphabet, the ' Indians would readily distinguish a new phenomenon like this, while to a ' native speaker, who had never known articulate sounds without it, it would ' almost necessarily be undetected.' Dr. Eitel well says, ' As to the number ' of tones at first used and their characteristics, it is perhaps impossible to say ' anything definite.' Minute investigations lead the native scholars to say there were three tones in existence at the time of the Shí King. The departing tone, it is said, not coming into use before the Chau dynasty, or, at least, not before the age of Confucius (551 B. C.).

This departing tone (去聲) was first noticed about A.D. 200—400. We give this statement for what it may be worth. Another Chinese writer considers this tone to have arisen about the fourth or fifth century of our era (Watters's *Essays on the Chinese Language*, p. 95). If this account of the tones at first having been few in number and added to in the course of centuries is true, we get a further step in the time of the Sung dynasty (A.D. 960—1341), when the philologists and lexicographers of those glorious days of Chinese literature, (when it attained its acme of excellence), proved that the four tones were divided into an upper and a lower series. In fact, the even tone was described, during the same dynasty, but about 200 years later than the former statement, to be divided into three—upper, middle and even.

It seems to have been left to foreigners to discover during the last fifty years that other tones existed in China besides the eight thus described above; and the credit of finding out the middle entering tone and the colloquial variants in tone is due to non-natives of China, as probably the first discovery of all of the tones in Chinese was made by Indians.

As the tones are the initial difficulty in learning Chinese, it is well that the beginner should have his attention drawn at the very first to them. PREMARE says: 'The mere sounds are, as it were, the body of the character, and the tones are in like manner the spirit.'* This description of the tones, at all events, contains a just appreciation of their importance. And that learned sinologue seems so thoroughly to understand the subject that his further descriptions of the matter form very good answers to the questions: What are the tones; and are they of any importance? To answer these questions let us take, for instance, the word 先 ₍ₑ₎sín, *before.* The sound is represented by the English spelling, *sin* (pronounced *seen*) and the tone by that little semi-circle, but insignificant as that little semi-circle is, yet a right understanding by a native of the word a European wishes to pronounce is as much conveyed by that little semi-circle as it is by the English letters *s i n.* Neglect that little sign and ignore the tone which it stands for, and the native is at a loss to know what the European means to say.

In other words, Chinese words may be compared to specimens, geological, botanical, or what you like, in a museum, and in this museum of Chinese ideas, it is necessary not only that the words, the specimens, should be arranged in cases or classes, similar in general characteristics, such as sound, but the differentiation of one from the other, which is already an accomplished fact, shall be represented in a manner to at once appeal to the ear. The methods of so distinguishing them is by the tones. These are the labels to the words to point out clearly what they are.

Tones then are used in this language, so largely monosyllabic that confusion would ensue but for their use. For example, let us take the sound *sin* (pronounced like the English word *seen*) again. That sound, amongst other ideas in the book language, stands in the colloquial for the words *before, ringworm,* and *thread,* but with a separate tone for each word, and

---

* 'Meri soni sunt litterarum quasi corpus; accentus autem sunt ipsis loco animæ.'
  PREMARE'S *Notitia Lingua Sinica,* p. 10.

written differently in the Chinese character. Now if the word ₍sín, meaning *before*, is pronounced in the same way as sín', meaning *thread*, it, of course, is no more the word *before*, but becomes the word *thread*, and *vice versâ*, or if it is pronounced ꞌsín, it means *ringworm*, and no more *thread* or *before*, or suppose the word is pronounced in some other tone, which does not belong to any word with that sound, no meaning is conveyed, or, to use an illustration, try to write English without any regard to spelling, and think that *scene* will do for *seen*, or *vice versâ*. It may be imagined how confusing and ludicrous it would be to hear a man talk about *ringworm* when he meant to talk about *thread*. Most ludicrous mistakes are constantly made by those who are just learning the tones, or who will not take the trouble to learn them.

When the learner has tried to speak Chinese for some time he will still find every now and then that something he has said falls flat on the ears of his listener, and see by his blank or perplexed face that it conveys no idea to his mind. In such a case the learner may think himself fortunate if some bystander, guessing at the idea, repeats words in the right tones, when a gleam of intelligence will replace the look of bewilderment on the face of the listener. A criterion of success in learning the tones will be found in the decrease in numbers of such failures in the course of time.

There are other helps it may be noted here, such as some words being aspirated and others not, and the context also helps to the understanding of the word, but, notwithstanding all other helps, the tone is of the utmost importance. As PREMARE rightly says:—' But if the sound simply were pronounced, no regard being had to the tone, or breathing' (the breathing being the aspirate) ' it would be impossible to determine its signification ; and indeed, it is the want of attention to this subject which occasions Europeans, after protracted labours devoted to the acquisition of this tongue, failing so often to be understood by the Chinese. They are learned, talented, and industrious, and yet can only stammer, through their whole lives, while at the same time some stupid Caffrarian, in a very short period, learns to speak as well as the Chinese themselves.' *

---

* The quotation in full in PREMARE is as follows:—' Exemplo sit littera 看 videre ; sonus quem ipsi dant sinæ est kꞌán, spiritus est asper kꞌan, accentus est rectus kꞌán, et interdum acutus kꞌán ; atque haec tria, scilicet sonus, spiritus et accentus sunt omnino necessaria. Cum vero sint aliae litterae aliud plane significantes, quae debent eodem modo pronunciari, evidens est quod etiamsi recte dicas kꞌán, tamen ex circumstantiis, hoc est, ex materia de qua sermo est, et ex his quae præcedunt vel sequuntur, plerumque colligunt sinæ quod vox illa quam profers significat videre. Et quid igitur esset, si duntaxat dicas kꞌan, nulla habita ratione nec ad spiritum kꞌan, nec ad accentum kꞌán atque haec est præcipua causa cur Europæi post tot labores in lingua sinica discenda positos a sinis vix intelligantur. Docti sunt, ingeniosi sunt, attenti sunt, et tamen per totam vitam plerique balbutiunt, interim dum stupidus aliquis cafer (sic) post tempus sat breve tam bene loquitur quam ipsimet sinae.'

PREMARE'S *Notitia Linguæ Sinicæ*, p. 10.

It is not learning nor talents that are a sure passport to an ability to acquire the tones, but more an ear gifted with, or trained to, a power of distinguishing between musical sounds, or a power of mimicry, a determination to succeed, accompanied with well-directed industrious efforts, which will generally assist a man in his acquisition of the tones. His success is more rapid and certain if he be blessed with a musical ear and a power of mimicry. A man should not, however, give up the attempt to learn the tones from an idea that he is not thus blessed. It is but few men that have not some idea of musical pitch, or the ability, if they will only try, to closely imitate what others say; and the continual attempt to do the latter, or detect the differences between the tones, will materially increase the ability to do both the one and the other, just as a man who exercises the muscles of his arms and legs, etc. in a properly directed manner is able after months of continual practice to pull an oar in a boat, in perfect time and accord with other rowers, in a manner which would astonish those who do not know what training will do. So training in the tones is bound to produce good results. The pity is that people get it into their heads that they can speak Chinese without knowing the tones. You might almost as well expect to be able to speak French without learning the French pronunciation, though do not be led away by the illustration to suppose that tones are the exact equivalent of pronunciation.

But still the question remains, What are tones? It is easy enough to say what they are not; for instance, they are not pronunciation, emphasis, or accent; but the difficulty consists in explaining to a European something which he knows nothing about, something to which there is nothing akin in his own language, or in the languages, which in the course of his education he has learned, be they dead, Classical languages, or living modern tongues, or, if there were, the knowledge of them has been lost.

This being the case it would, perhaps, have been as well, as Dr. WILLIAMS says, if the Chinese name for them, *shing*, had been adopted into our language instead of using a word, such as *tone*, which conveys other ideas to our minds.

It is very much as if a race of mankind, say in the centre of New Guinea, were to be discovered, who had a new sense, that is to say, a sense which the rest of mankind were not endowed with. It would be well nigh impossible to describe this sense to the rest of mankind, who had not seen the effects it produced and what it was, and any attempts at description would be in many cases misleading, for those who heard the description would be inclined to follow the illustrations out in their entirety, and thus misunderstand what was being attempted to be explained to them.

Tones then may be said to be certain positions or inflections of the voice which are used for certain words, each word having its own tone, or in many cases two, which are used at different times. These positions into which the voice is put for words are various in their character. The position is for certain tones a level or sustained modulation, the difference between the tones belonging to this class being one of musical pitch. For others it is a rising modulation of the voice; as if when a violin bow were being drawn across a string of the violin the finger of the player should slide from a lower note to a higher;—the difference between the tones belonging to this class being in the amount of rising modulation the voice undergoes. Another class, a diminishing, receding modulation of the voice; the difference between the tones comprised in this class being, as in some of the others, a high or low one. And there is yet another class which has been described as an evanescent modulation, the tones in this class being distinguished from each other by the musical pitch.

If the beginner could only put himself into the same position that a child seems to be in when learning Chinese, there doubtless would be no difficulty at all in the tones. A European child in infancy, given equal facilities, learns Chinese, bristling with difficulties as it appears to adults, more readily, and, if anything, more correctly than his or her mother tongue. What is the reason of this? The language is, as a general rule, more natural and logical in its construction, or rather the Chinese mind is more natural and logical in its sequence of ideas, and consequently the Chinese language is more logical in the manner of putting ideas; furthermore, a monosyllabic language, or at all events with regard to Chinese, one which is to a great extent monosyllabic, it is natural to suppose would be more readily apprehended by a child's mind. Besides these two great advantages there is the further advantage of tone, to which a child is naturally inclined, and it is only by education that an infant learns that tone is unnecessary in a European language. A Chinese child never learns this, and, having originally, in common with its European cousin, copied the exact tone in which it hears a word first pronounced, adheres to this original pronunciation of the tone, assisted materially by the fact that it hears this word pronounced in no other way, or tone, while its cousin, the European child, while acquiring its own language, at first adheres to the original tone in which a word has been first pronounced, and persists in this adherence for some time, as a general rule, till it gets confused by hearing a multiplicity of tones given to the same word and eventually finds it is useless to battle for a language in its infant state when his superiors have long ago decided that the language has outgrown its infantile state, and eventually yields to the force of circumstances and, copying the example of his elders, forgets that there is such a thing as tone at all.

How is it possible for a European adult to place himself in the same position as regards tones as a child would be in? Clearly he cannot place himself in precisely the same position, as he has already the experience of his own and probably other languages, which at the present day are wanting in tones, to mislead him. Let him, however, try and get as near the child's position in this respect, at least, as he can. Listen acutely to the tone that his teacher pronounces a word in, repeat it after him and re-repeat it and go on a hundred times—a thousand, if necessary, till the exact tone has been got, and do this with every new word. More pains are necessary for the adult than for the child, as to the child the tone is everything, while to the adult it is nothing. Repeat the same plan with every new word learned, and surely such infinite pains will not have been spent in vain. Being unfortunately an adult the learner ought also to use his superior abilities and previous knowledge as a vantage ground for further attainments by, for one thing, having a formula, shall we call it? Such, for instance as, ₍sín ʻsín sín' sít₀, ₍lín ˢlín lín² lít₂, and with each new word finding from enquiry, or better still from the dictionary, the correct tone, then trying to say it in exactly the same tone as the same toned word in the formula, but he should not be content with supposing that be has it correct, he should test it with his teacher and bother him with questions as to whether he is perfectly correct or not, and not be content with anything short of *perfection*. He may think it is not of much importance and the teacher will probably think that the pupil being a European he cannot ever learn Chinese perfectly correctly, especially if after several attempts at a word he makes very bad shots at it, but other Europeans have learned to speak Chinese, and amongst them have been some who have approximated very closely to the Chinese in their tones, so close that much of what they said might be supposed to be uttered by Chinese. If others have attained to such an excellence, why should not he? At all events he will not unless he tries. And it is well worth the trial, as he will know when he has attained to this excellence.

All this trouble and painstaking when he is in his study, and on the learning of every new word; but when he goes out to exercise his hard-acquired knowledge he should not cramp himself by constant thoughts as to the tone of every word in the sentence he utters, any more than he would bend his head down and watch every step he took when walking. Speech must come freely from his mouth, and he must not hesitate over, and examine, every word mentally before it issues from his lips, or he will never speak freely. A general and his officers do not minutely inspect each soldier to see as they issue out for the attack whether their uniform and accoutrements are all right; that has to be done at drill. The learner should never cease to drill himself in tones for many a long day after his first start.

Methods of Describing Tones.

Different methods have been used to try and convey to the foreign mind, unacquainted with tones, an idea of what they are. To depend only upon these descriptions to acquire a knowledge of the tones would be but of little use, as tones in their correctness are only to be learned from the native pronunciation of them, but these descriptions may assist the learner, supplemented by hearing them pronounced, to a correct knowledge of what they are, imperfect though such methods may be by themselves alone for conveying a perfectly correct idea of the tones to one who is previously unacquainted with them. One way of describing the tones has been to compare them to the inflections of voice, which are used in certain passages properly read and emphasised, or in speech properly inflected in its utterance. When this explanation is given it must not be supposed that the same words, as a rule, are capable of having different tones applied to them just as in English words may have a different emphasis, owing simply to their position in the sentence, or the exigencies of the case, such as the emotions the speaker desires to give expression to, or from the inflexion of his voice—such are intonation and expression—not Chinese Tones; for Chinese words are capable of intonation of voice and emphasis, which can be thrown into the voice without, though it may seem strange to those unacquainted with the fact, interfering with the *pitch* of the tone, and this brings us to another way in which it has been attempted to make the tonic system intelligible to the foreigner, viz.:—by comparing the tones to musical notes.

List of Tones.

The following is a list of the nine primary tones in Cantonese : -

Upper Series	*Middle Tone*	*Lower Series.*
上平 Shŏng² ₍p'ing	中入 ₍Chung yap₎	下平 Há² ₍p'ing.
上上 Shŏng² ˁshŏng.		下上 Há² ˁshŏng
上去 Shŏng² höü⁾		下去 Há² höü⁾
上入 Shŏng² yap₎		下入 Há² yap₎

' The degree in which these two series' (that is the upper and lower series) ' vary from each other is not the same in all tones; the upper and lower *p'ing shing* being distinctly marked while there is very little perceptible difference between the upper and lower *shŏng shing*.'

WILLIAMS'S *Easy Lessons in Chinese*, p. 49.

Division of the Tones.

These tones are classed together in different ways, such as those of the Upper and Lower Series, which together make the 8 tones into which the Cantonese, as a rule, say the words in their language are divided, and which are the only tones appearing in the majority of dictionaries.

These eight tones are divided by the Chinese again into correct and deflected, or 平 ͬp'ing and 仄 chak ͬ, the first of each series belonging to the former and the others being classed under the deflected.

These eight tones are further divided into the :—

平 ͬp'ing. *or* Even tones

上 shöng². *or* Rising tones

去 höü³. *or* Receding tones

入 yap₂. *or* Entering tones

This classification is so simple that there is no need for offering any remarks on it.

Description of the Tones.

'The 平聲 ͬp'ing ͬshing is precisely the musical monotone, pronounced without elevation or depression' (at the beginning,) 'being the natural unconstrained expression of the voice. ⁛ * Thus in the sentences :—

I am going to town; *I hope it will not* rain; *You must look and* see;

if the last word in each is sounded in somewhat of a dissatisfied or commanding tone, higher than the other words, the previous part of the sentence will naturally fall in the ͬp'ing ͬshing. In questions, uttered in a pleasant inviting tone, the words preceding the last naturally fall in the upper ͬp'ing ͬshing, as:—

Will you let me see it ? *Will you come* too ?'

But though this is the case and it commences high in the musical scale, it has an abrupt fall which withal is so rapid that it is only of late that it has been noticed.

' The negative answer to such questions (spoken by the same voice) would naturally fall into the lower ͬp'ing ͬshing, as:—

When I asked him, ' Will you let me see it ?' he said, ' No, I'll do no such thing. '

' Here the different cadence of the question and reply illustrate the upper and lower ͬp'ing ͬshing.'—WILLIAMS'S *Easy Lessons in Chinese*, p. 49.

Here again is a fall in this tone at its end which likewise has never been noticed till lately. This fall in even tones, it may be remarked, is really a natural fall in the voice, which occurs when an even sustained note is sounded. When a number of such tones follow one after the other, the voice drops at the end of the sentence, or before giving utterance to a different tone.

There is, however, a second, or Higher, Upper Even Tone into which some words are put and which also at times shows past tense, etc. This second, or 上平變音 shöng² ͜p'ing p'ín' ͜yam, the P'ín Tone of the Upper Even Tone, is found in the following words, for example :—

貓 ͜máu, *a cat*, and 鎗 ͜ts'öng, *a gun*.

'It partakes of the nature of a slight shriek,' differing not only in musical pitch (being nearer to the 上 平 shöng² ͜p'ing, Upper Even Tone, in that respect than to the 下 平 há² ͜p'ing, Lower Even Tone), from the other two Even Tones, but also in the manner of its pronunciation, it having 'a certain quickness or jerkiness of pronunciation.'—PARKER in *Overland China Mail.*

There is nearly an octave's difference between the two Even Tones, the 上 平 shöng² ͜p'ing, Upper Even Tone, and the 下 平 há² ͜p'ing, Lower Even Tone, while the Higher Upper Even Tone is more than an octave above the Lower Even.

These Lower Even Toned words seem to give a stability and character to the Cantonese; they are full and rich, and a European who has a full toned voice generally speaks Cantonese better than one with a weak piping voice, at all events Cantonese from his lips sounds better than from those of the other man.

There is no doubt this tone, the 上平變音 shöng² ͜p'ing p'ín' ͜yam, the P'ín Tone of the Even Tone, does exist, and the beginner will do well to keep his ears open for it, though, strange to say, to the average European ear it is so subtle as not to be distinguished, obtuse in this sense as most Europeans have become from speaking a language in which tone is of no account. And here consists the fallacy of learning Chinese by simply learning what the tones of a word are, that is to say, learning that a certain word is in the 上 平 shöng² ͜p'ing, or Upper Even Tone, for example, instead of first learning to pronounce the word properly, and then bracing yourself up to that pronunciation by comparing it with other words in that same tone and then finally fixing in your memory that it belongs to that tone, the

上平 shöng² ͵p'ing, Upper Even Tone; for, supposing you learn first that it belongs to this tone class instead of making a point of pronouncing it properly first, you run away at once with the idea that it is a 上平 shöng² ͵p'ing, Upper Even Tone, and it is possible that it is a 上平變音 shöng² ͵p'ing p'ín᾿ ͵yam, the P'ín Tone of the Upper Even Tone. If you have a good ear and good powers of mimicry, great points of advantage in learning Chinese, you run a good chance of learning the word in the right tone; then it is possible you may detect the difference on coming to compare it with other words that are really in the 上平 shöng² ͵p'ing, Upper Even Tone. At all events, keep your ear open for these distinctions between the 上平 shöng² ͵p'ing, Upper Even, and 上平變音 shöng² ͵p'ing p'ín᾿ ͵yam, the P'ín Tone of the Upper Even Tone, for no dictionary yet published gives all the words, which should be in the 上平變音 shöng² ͵p'ing p'ín᾿ ͵yam, the P'ín Tone of the Upper Even Tone, in that Tone. Dr. EITEL puts a few of them into his dictionary. Do not consider such distinctions hypercritical, or a waste of time. The disposition to do so has made some learned Sinologues commit such egregious errors as to entirely ignore a well marked Tone, the 中入 ͵chung yap₂ the Medial Entering Tone, of which we shall speak presently. These distinctions do exist, subtle as they may seem to you, and while not distressing yourself with them too much, at the same time try to train your ear to distinguish them. There is no reason why you should not try to speak Chinese properly, and if you make the effort you may find that you will succeed better than you thought at first, and it is possible that eventually you may be able, after a sufficient lengthened course of study, to distinguish some more of these subtle distinctions which are still believed to be lurking about in Cantonese, but which have not yet been brought to book, more's the pity.

'The 上聲 *shöng²* ͵*shing*,' (Rising Tone,) 'is a rising inflection of the voice ending higher than it began, such as is heard in the direct question, pronounced in somewhat of a high, shrill tone;—"*it loudly calls, vehement, ardent, strong.*" It is also heard in exclamatory words, as, *ah! Can it be!* The last word of the preceding sentences are in the 上聲 *shöng²* ͵*shing*,' (Rising Tone).—WILLIAMS's *Easy Lessons in Chinese*, p. 50.

With regard to the difference between the 上上 shöng² ⸂shöng, Upper Rising Tone, and 下上 há² ⸂shöng, Lower Rising Tone, the following state-ment will give an idea:—'the Upper Rising Tone gradually ascends, altering its pitch about half a tone while the syllable is being uttered with a steadily waxing intensity of effort, ⁎ ⁎ the Lower Rising Tone starts from a lower pitch, does not ascend so high as the other and suddenly breaks off with a sort of jerk or circumflex.'—EITEL's *Chinese Dictionary in the Cantonese Dialect*, Introduction, p. xxix.

What has been called the Third Rising Tone really consists of five or more different tones. Every word that is used in these tones belongs originally to another tone, being used in this other tone as well. Nearly all the tones contribute words which are occasionally, or often, as the case may be, used in Rising Tones. The words most generally put into these tones are Nouns, 'familiar words in the Lower Departing Tone (or 下去 há^2 höü^2). It often happens also that words in the Lower Even Tone, or 下平 há^2 ͻp'ing, are put into these Rising Tones. Occasionally words in the Upper Departing Tone, or 上去 shöng^2 höü^2 are likewise put into these Tones. Words in the two Rising Tones, 上聲 shöng^2 ͻshing, are put into these Tones, as well, but not quite as often.' The Upper Even Tone, 上平 shöng^2 ͻp'ing, however, never contributes words to these Rising Tones for the very good reason that this tone has a variant tone which is not a Rising Tone, viz., the Higher Upper Even Tone. It must be remembered that in reading this changing from the other tones into these Rising Tones never happens, it is only in conversation. It is a little misleading to say that these Rising Tones are adopted when a word ends a sentence. They do undoubtedly end a sentence at times.

The Rising Tones are used when the word stands alone, but when it is used in combination it often takes its original tone, as :— 渡 tò^5⁎ (original tone tò^2) but when used with 船 ͻshün, *a boat*, it reverts to its original tone, as :—渡船 tò^2 ͻshün, *a passage boat*.

The Rising Tones, or rather the variants, are also used as a sign of past time—of an action being accomplished, as :—

叫佢嚟 kíü^2 ᶜk·öü ͻlai, *tell him to come.* 嚟咯 ͻlaí· lok ͻ, *he has come.*
佢嚟囉咩 ᶜk·öü ͻlaí· lo^2 ͻme? *He has come, has he?* 嚟咯 ͻlaí· lok ͻ, *yes.*

But rules for the use of these, and the other variant tones are given more fully further on.

'The 去聲 *höü^2* ͻshing, Departing Tone, is a prolonged tone, diminishing while it is uttered, just as a diminuendo, or an inverted swell, does in music, and sounded somewhat gruffly. The Chinese say that it is " clear, distinct, its dull, low path is long ; " and they call it the *departing* tone, because it goes away like flowing water never to return. It is the converse of the 上聲 *shŏng² ₍shing*, ending lower than it began. The 下去 há² höü', Lower Departing Tone, is nearer a monotone, not so gruff as the 上去 shŏng² höü', Upper Departing Tone. The drawling tone of repressed discontent, as when one calls, but is still afraid of offending and ekes out the sound, may perhaps illustrate this tone.'—WILLIAMS's *Easy Lessons in Chinese*, p. 50.

There is no difficulty in knowing what words belong to the fourth Tone Class, as all words that end in k, p, and t belong to it. ‘They further differ from all the other tones by a peculiar abruptness of enunciation.'—EITEL's *Chinese Dictionary in the Cantonese Dialect*, Introduction, p. xxix. There are three well defined tones belonging to this class, the 上 shŏng², 中 ₍chung, and 下 há², Upper, Middle, and Lower, 入 yap₂, or Entering Tones. There is also some assistance to be derived from the fact that most of the words having long vowels belong to the 中入 ₍chung yap₂, Middle Entering Tone. The others, as well as some words with long vowels, belong to the 上入 shŏng² yap₂, Upper Entering Tone, or 下入 há² yap₂, Lower Entering Tone.

· The correct application of the tones to every word in speaking or reading is the principal difficulty with which the beginner has to contend. In English they are all heard in conversation every day, according to the different humours of people or their peculiar mode of enunciation ; but in that language, tones of words never affect the meaning of the speaker, except so far as they indicate his feelings ; and, moreover, they are applied to sentences rather than to isolated words. In Chinese, on the contrary, the tones are applied to every word, and have nothing to do either with accent or emphasis ; in asking or answering, entreating or refusing, railing or flattering, soothing or recriminating, they remain ever the same. The unlettered native knows almost nothing of the learned distinctions into tones, but he attends to them closely himself, and detects a mispronunciation as soon as the learned man, while he is much less likely to catch a foreigner's meaning.'

The Variant Tones.

It is as well to acknowledge at once that there are nine primary tones in Cantonese, and only nine in the book language ; and that there are, besides these, nine secondary tones as well, but not in the book language.

However, see below as to how these latter nine may be simplified in practice.

To those who may still persist in ignoring the number of these tones it may be well to quote Mr. PARKER (*China Review*, Vol. 8, p. 366), whose word is law on the matter of Chinese tones. He says: 'Besides the nine regular Cantonese tones, there are, in short, nine corresponding variable tones.' In fact, each of the nine tones has a tone into which it is changed sometimes well-nigh permanently in conversation, at other times always when used in certain connections, or to convey certain meanings.

Though, however, each of the nine tones has a variant tone, yet their classification is apparently capable of simplification, as the variant of the upper retiring tone (Mr. CHAN's middle retiring) and of the middle entering tone are the same; again, that of the upper rising is nearly the same, the voice lingering longer, however, on the tone at the end. Once more one tone serves equally well as the variant of the lower retiring and the lower entering tones; this tone one would feel inclined to describe as smooth in its progress upwards. Again the variant for the lower rising is almost similar to it, but its distinctive feature lies in more emphasis being thrown into its pronunciation, especially in its inception and first rising; for the voice seems to seize on it with avidity, lingering on it, and a crescendo effect comes in, in its middle course, dying away towards its end. Then though the variant of the upper even and the upper entering tone are very much alike, there is a difference between them, the latter is lengthened in its pronunciation and not abrupt as the former, the voice lingers on it and gives emphasis to it with almost, if not quite, a crescendo effect. Of all these variants, the one which appeals most to the learner is the variant of the lower even: it is so marked and distinctive in its character that it has hitherto well nigh monopolised the attention and taken the other variant rising tones under its own name, or, at all events, the distinction between these five, or more, rising variant tones has not been pointed out, or clearly defined, and they have all been considered by many as one and the same tone. It will be noticed that this has a distinct fall and a long rise, in fact, being the most prolonged of any of the rising tones, and much emphasis is thrown into the voice on its recovery from the fall, increasing in its volume as it rises into a good crescendo and dying away at the end again. It is a tone that is bound to force itself on the attention of the hearer who has the slightest acuteness of ear for tones.

From the above it will be seen that what has been described previously as the Third Rising Tone is properly divisible into at least, if not possibly more, five separate Rising Tones, all of which, if the learner wishes to speak

Cantonese perfectly, should be learned from a good teacher, who speaks correct Cantonese.

The Higher Upper Even Tone has already been described.

The variant tone of the 上入 shŏng² yap, Upper Entering Tone is a prolongation of that tone.

As an instance of the use of these variant tones in forming new words or shades of meaning the word 大 tái², great, may be called attention to. Tái² in the Lower Retiring means big, large, great, e.g.:—

(1) 一個大人 yat, ko⁹ tái² ₍yan, a big man, a grown up person, (also 大人 is a title for high officials such as Your, or His, Excellency, Your, or His, Honour, etc., etc.).

(2) Tái⁵*, i.e., in the Variant Rising Tone of the Lower Retiring as in the phrase 你大個嗰時 ⁵néí tái⁵* ko⁹ ⁶ko ₍shí, when you have grown up. Here the variant tone shows the growing up being attained or looked forward to. Without its use, when that meaning was to be conveyed, the phrase would fall flat and tame.

(3) ₒTái in the Higher Upper Even Tone as in the phrase 啲咁大 個 tik, kòm⁹ ₒtái ko⁹, a tiny mite, 你啲咁大個嗰陣時 ⁵néí tik, kòm⁹ ₒtái ko⁹ ⁶ko chan² ₍shí, when you were a little mite of a child.

Again take 話 wá², to speak, and 口話 wa⁵* patois, dialect, language ; the one in the Lower Retiring Tone ; the other in the Variant Tone of the Lower Retiring.

As another instance of the differentiation produced by the use of these variant tones, take the word Honam, the name given to the suburb of Canton situated on the south side of the river. This word as applied to the locality is always in its original tones, but the last syllable is put into the variant when the steamer so-called is mentioned. This is no fancy, but established usage, though it happens that, very rarely, the original tones are used for the steamer.

These are only a few instances of the innumerable examples of the change of meaning and tense shown by the use of these variant tones.

An interesting set of rules and examples of the use of these variant tones was published in the ' *China Review*,' Vol. XXIV., pp. 209-226, by Mr. Cʜ'ᴀᴜ Cʜᴀɴ Sᴇɴᴇ, with Prefatory Remarks by the present author. It may be laid down—

(1) That verbs in the Perfect Tense take variant tones when words such as 嘵 ₍híú or 嗰 ʻcho are not used to convey the idea of past time.

(2) That ' the Present Participles of Intransitive Verbs of attitude or appearance ' take variant tones.

(3) When the word —— with the meaning of one or a is used between two words, generally verbs, as, for example, in phrases like ' " bite a bite " out of it,' then the —— yat₍ (shortened in Chinese into ₍á) is in the Higher Upper Even Tone, and when, as is often the case, the a is dropped out, the second word takes the variant which belongs to its original tone.

(4) After 幾 ʻkéí, how, 咁 kòm', so, and the phrases 冇幾 ʻmo · ʻkéí and 唔係幾 ₍m haí² ʻkéí, not very, words representing dimensions or qualities take a variant tone often.

(5) Words duplicated for emphasis—not nouns, but generally adverbs—take a variant tone for the first of these double words.

(6) But when some adjectives and adverbs are duplicated to minimise the sense, the last word of the two takes a variant tone, and these ' are generally followed ' by the word 哋 téí².

(7) Adverbs formed by the duplication of a word take a variant tone in the latter of the two words.

(8) The common names of things or places and of occupations of individuals and relationships commonly used take a variant tone. If a single character, the character takes it ; but if the name, etc., is formed of two or more characters, only the last character takes the variant.

(9) The names of steamers in most cases take a variant tone in the last character of their names when these characters are originally in the Upper or Lower Even, or Upper Retiring Tone, but not when in the Upper Rising or Upper Entering Tones.

(10) Proper names of persons and places take a variant in the last character often : but it is often more respectful to persons to use the original tones.

(11) Certain words which do not come under the above rules are always in a variant tone in the colloquial, as 都 ₀tò, 嘀 ₀ti.

(12) Many of the Upper Even Tone Finals can be used either in that tone or in the Higher Upper Even (variant) as the sense to be conveyed by them demands. Be somewhat sparing of putting finals into a variant in the middle of a series of sentences unless the sense really demands it.

(13) As to whether certain words shall go into a variant tone depends often, unless the word is one which must be in a variant, on euphony, or the rhythmic flow of the sentence.

Marks to designate the Tones.

It must be remembered that Chinese books are not marked with the tones ; an educated native knows the right tones of the words as they occur in the books. It is only when a word is in a tone which is not the common tone of the word that it is marked, and the method by which this is done is to make a little circle at one of the four corners of the character. Each corner has its appropriate tones assigned to it. The left hand lower corner being appropriated to the 平 ₍p'ing, or even tones, the left hand upper to the 上 shöng², or rising tones. the right hand upper to the 去 höü', or receding tones, and the right hand lower corner to the 入 yap₂, or entering tones. These are the only signs that the Chinese use, and this only when it is absolutely necessary that they should be used. It will be seen that there is no distinction in the native signs employed between the different tones which belong to the same class, that is to say a 上平 shöng² ₍p'ing, Upper Even, and 下平 há² ₍p'ing, Lower Even, are both represented by the same tonal mark. No difficulty, however, arises from this paucity of tone marks, as far as the Chinese are themselves concerned, for, as has been already stated, these tonic marks are but seldom used, only occurring a few times, if as often as that, in the course of as many pages ; and, furthermore, if those few words are occasionally used in another tone, as a rule it is but one other tone that they are used in, therefore no ambiguity is likely to arise. The case is, however, very different when we come to deal with foreigners, such as Europeans, learning the Chinese language ; for here we have those who do not know by conversational practice from infancy upwards, and from an educational course extending over many years the correct tones for each word ; and yet again as an additional reason, when a foreigner desires to write out the sounds of the Chinese words, transliterating them into his own alphabet, as he best can, he has a number of Chinese words, groups of which are represented by the same spelling in a foreign language, so many words belonging to each group that the foreigner is confused, more especially at the beginning of his course of study, as to which Chinese word a combination of English letters is intended to represent. The context will show what many of the words so spelled represent, but in some cases this requires thought, and it is, therefore, taking the whole subject into consideration, best that each word so written should be accompanied by a tonal mark, which shall represent, accurately, intelligibly, and in a manner easily to be apprehended, the tone to which the word belongs. The above remarks will show the reasons for books prepared for those who wish to learn Chinese bristling with tonic marks, and the man who wishes to learn Chinese thoroughly and properly will find that in the long run he gets on better with such a book, and makes more real progress than he does with another, though the other may be more useful, if rightly used, to the tourist or to the man who has not the time nor the inclination to learn more than a smattering of Chinese.

We come now to the methods used by foreigners to represent the tones. Some have endeavoured to show tones by ' marking the vowels with different accents.' This is a confusing method, except to those intimately acquainted with it, as it is the most natural course to utilise such marks to represent the value of the vowels, as is done in our English dictionaries, and use extraordinary signs to represent what is an extraordinary incident of words — to use signs not used by us in English to represent tones which are unknown to us in English,—and moreover such a method of representing the tones has not been employed by foreigners writing books in Cantonese till quite recently, and it is better to stick to the established usage when that established usage is the better plan. The effect of using the contrary plan is that an awkward arrangement is arrived at of marking over the vowels their quantities or powers as well as the tone of the word, or else nearly all ' prosodical marks affecting the vowels ' have to be left out and the next step arrived at is to leave out the tonic marks entirely—a process of evolution, or rather of retrogression, eminently unsatisfactory. Another objection is that it would lead beginners to suppose that the tone was connected with the vowel. The vowel no doubt has sometimes something to do with the tone, but not to such an extent as one would naturally infer from such a method of distinguishing the tones.

Another method is that of marking the tones by figures. We have already said that, though pretty well adapted for Pekingese with its paucity of tones, it would be inconvenient for Cantonese with its eleven or more tones.

Marks of apostrophy have also been used in some of the dialects, but it will be readily seen that there is not sufficient material to use for such a purpose.

In the Hakka, as written by the German missionaries, there is also another system employed, which consists in putting acute and grave accents at different corners of the words, in some cases with a straight short dash underneath the accent as well. Again in Hakka the tones are but few in number, and such arrangements are more easily used than they would be in Cantonese, besides which these marks have never been used in Cantonese, and there is no type available even supposing it were a good plan for Cantonese.

There is yet again another method, which has been employed in Cantonese by Dr. CHALMERS, which consists of a combination of one of the above modes with a new plan of using different type, and a leaving out of the tonic marks when the word ends in those consonants which show that it belongs to a certain tone class. This method has not been adopted by anyone else. It is no doubt very convenient considered from a typographical point of view, but it seems a more regular and systematic way to give every word its tonic mark.

And lastly there is the modification of the native method of representing the tones, which was first used in BRIDGMAN's *Chrestomathy*, and has continued to be used up to the present day by nearly all who have written books dealing with the Cantonese dialect, amongst whom may be mentioned WILLIAMS, LOBSCHIED, KERR, and EITEL. It is the system adopted in this book. This method has several advantages over the others. All the other methods are strange and unknown to the Chinese. The learner would, in using the others, require to tell his teacher what tone such and such things were meant to represent, and such telling would be of little use with regard to some of the marks that are used in some of the modes employed to represent the tones in Chinese. Of course in the majority of cases the teacher can tell the tone from the character, but in some cases it is well that the teacher should be able to see himself how the tone is marked. In this system likewise every word is marked with its tone, and it occasionally happens that some of the words which by Dr. CHALMERS' system are left unmarked go in Colloquial into a rising, variant tone. These marks in this method are as applicable to the Chinese character as to the English spelled word, which represents that character, but figures and accents cannot well be printed along with the Chinese characters. This method is applicable to any dialect in China, and it is a thousand pities that, when such an admirable system is in use, it has not been availed of by foreigners for all the Chinese languages, which have been treated of in books instead of different systems being in use for different so-called dialects, thus increasing the difficulty of learning them when the difficulties are sufficiently great without being added to. It unfortunately even happens that in some dialects even more than one system is in use.

This system as has already been stated is an adaptation of the native system, the semi-circle being used for the upper series of tones, and the semi-circle with a short dash underneath it to represent the lower series, as, for example :—

上平 shŏng² ₵p'ing, Upper Even, as :—₵sin.   下平 há² ₵p'ing, Lower Even, as :—₵lin.

上上 shŏng² ᶜshŏng, Upper Rising, as :—ᶜsin.   下上 há² ᶜshŏng, Lower Rising, as :—ᶜlin.

上去 shŏng² höü', Upper Retreating, as:—sin'.   下去 há² höü', Lower Retreating, as :—lin².

上入 shŏng² yap₂, Upper Entering, as :—pit₎.   下入 há² yap₂, Lower Entering, as :—lit₎.

There now remain the other tones to be dealt with, viz. :—the 上平 變音 shŏng² ₵p'ing p'ín' ₵yam, the 中入 ₵chung yap₂, Medial Departing Tone, and the variant tones. The 上平變音 shŏng² ₵p'ing p'ín' ₵yam, Upper Even P'ín Tone, is represented by PARKER and EITEL by a circle in the 平 ₵p'ing position as ₒmáú, being an adoption of a Siamese tone mark, and it is the plan likewise adopted in this book.

The same plan is likewise used for the 中入 ₵chung yap₂, Medial Departing Tone, viz. :—a circle, but of course at the 入 yap₂ position, as :—pokₒ.

There now remain the Rising Tones. These have generally been represented by their own tone marks reversed, and an asterisk placed at the right hand upper corner of the word.

In this book this asterisk is employed, as it is useful in showing that the word is in a different tone in the colloquial from what it is in the book language. It is unsatisfactory to group all these Variant Rising Tones together. It is better that the Tonic Mark should show distinctly the tone of the word, and the asterisk be reserved alone to show that the tone is a different one to the original tone, and not to show what the tone is.

To recapitulate, the following method has been used to represent the variant tones :—The Higher Upper Even Tone, the 上平變音 shŏng² ₵p'ing p'ín' ₵yam, has already been represented by other writers by a circle at the lower left hand corner of the word, as ₒsün. It is also the sign used in this book. The majority of the other tones are represented in this book by the turning of the usual tone sign upside down as shown in the page set aside for ' Tonic

Marks and Abbreviations used in this Book.' The only exception besides that of the Higher Upper Even tone, already mentioned, are the variants of the Middle Entering Tone (the 中入變音 ₍chung yap₂ p‘in³ ₍yam) of the Upper Rising, and the Upper Retiring. In the case of the variant of the Middle Entering, in addition to the small circle, the sign of the ordinary ₍chung yap₂, a figure one is added (see page mentioned above). As regards the other two variants, the Upper Rising one and the Upper Retiring, the sign which was formerly used for the so-called third rising tone is employed, placed at the proper corners of the words. The page mentioned above will make this plain.

Tonic Exercises.

Go through the following Tonic Exercises every day regularly for three months at least.

Let your teacher read each set to you and then repeat them after him. He will read the first line in the First Series to you and then the first line in the Second Series. The meanings of the words are simply given to satisfy any laudable curiosity the learner may have as to the meanings of the words he is repeating so often. In this way it often happens that the meaning of many words are learned without the learner actually setting himself down with the express object of learning them.

This drudgery must be gone through most conscientiously and thoroughly, not considering that you have done your duty until you have gone through each set dozens or scores of times every day; for these voice and ear exercises are as important as finger exercises are to the learner on the piano.

' It cannot, however, be too strongly impressed upon learners from the outset that both aspirates and tones are of the utmost importance to one who would learn to speak Chinese intelligibly. ✳ ✳ ✳ ✳ ✳ ✳ ✳ ✳ ✳ ✳ ✳ ✳ ✳ The distinction of tones in Chinese often appears to beginners to make the acquisition of the spoken language almost hopelessly difficult, but this difficulty, like many others, is found to yield to persevering effort, and by constantly reading aloud after a teacher, the ear becomes familiar with the difference in the tones of the words pronounced. At the same time it is not desirable to trust to the ear alone in trying to remember what is the tone of a particular word. A Chinese child will unconsciously acquire the right tones in speaking, and use them without any effort of memory all through life in the same way a foreign child learns and uses the correct tones; but, with the rarest possible exceptions, foreign adults will find it necessary to learn what the proper tone of each character is, together with its sound and meaning. Both tones and aspirates are chiefly important in the spoken language, but even in studying the written language it is necessary to notice that a character often has two sounds, one aspirated and the other unaspirated, or one of one tone and another of another, and its shade of meaning varies accordingly ; thus, the word 中 " the middle " is differently pronounced when it means " to hit the centre." '—FOSTER's *Elementary Lessons in Chinese.*

First Series, Comprising the Upper Tones.

	Shöng² ͨp'ing	Shöng² ͨshöng	Shöng² höü³	Shöng² & ͨChung yap₂	Meaning of the Words.
	1	2	3	4	
1	先蘚線屑	ͨSín	ͨSín	Sín⁾	Sít ͺ	Before, moss, thread, bits
2	威偉畏	ͨWaí	ͨWaí	Waí⁾		Dignity, great, awe.
3	幾紀記	ͨKéí	ͨKéí	Kéí⁾		Several, to record, to remember.
4	諸主著拙	ͨChü	ͨChü	Chü⁾	Chüt ͺ	All, master, to publish, stupid
5	修叟秀	ͨSaú	ͨSaú	Saú⁾		Adorn, venerable man, elegant
6	東董凍篤	ͨTung	ͨTung	Tung⁾	Tuk ͺ	East, to rule, cold, real.
7	英影應益	ͨYing	ͨYing	Ying⁾	Yik ͺ	Excellent, shadow, answer, beneficial
8	賓稟儐畢	ͨPan	ͨPan	Pan⁾	Pat ͺ	Guest, petition, Imperial concubine, ended.
9	張掌帳着	ͨChöng	ͨChöng	Chöng⁾	Chök ͺ	To draw out, palm of the hand, curtain, to order.
10	剛講絳角	ͨKong	ͨKong	Kong⁾	Kok ͺ	Strong, to speak, to descend, horn.
11	朝沼照	ͨChíú	ͨChíú	Chíú⁾		Morning, pool, to illumine
12	泒古故	ͨKwú	ͨKwú	Kwú⁾		Alone, ancient, old.
13	鴛婉怨乙	ͨYün	ͨYün	Yün⁾	yüt ͺ	Drake, yielding, animosity, curved.
14	皆解介	ͨKáí	ͨKáí	Káí⁾		All, to open, firm or uncorrupted.
15	登等凳德	ͨTang	ͨTang	Tang⁾	Tak ͺ	Ascend, sort, stool, virtue.
16	師史四	ͨSz	ͨSz	Sz⁾		Master, history, four
17	金錦禁急	ͨKam	ͨKam	Kam⁾	Kap ͺ	Metal, embroidery, prohibit, hasty.
18	交絞教	ͨKáú	ͨKáú	Káú⁾		Intercourse, to strangle, to teach.
19	栽宰載	ͨTsoí	ͨTsoí	Tsoí⁾		To plant, to rule, to contain.
20	雖髓歲	ͨSöü	ͨSöü	Söü⁾		Although, marrow, year.
21	兼檢劍劫	ͨKím	ͨKím	Kím⁾	Kíp ͺ	Joined, to examine, sword, to rob.
22	津贐進卒	ͨTsun	ͨTsun	Tsun⁾	Tsut ͺ	A ford, presents, to enter, soldiers
23	科火貨	ͨFo	ͨFo	Fo⁾		Order or sort, fire, cargo.
24	緘減鑒甲	ͨKám	ͨKám	Kám⁾	Káp ͺ	To bind, to diminish, mirror, armour
25	翻反泛發	ͨFán	ͨFán	Fán⁾	Fát ͺ	To fly, to rebel, to float, to issue.
26	家假嫁㗆	ͨKá	ͨKá	Ká⁾	Kák ͺ	Family, false, to marry (a husband), gradation.
27	官管貫括	ͨKwún	ͨKwún	Kwún⁾	Kwut ͺ	Officer, tube, to connect, to inclose.
28	魁賄誨	ͨFúí	ͨFúí	Fúí⁾		Headmost, a bribe, to teach.
29	遮者蔗隻	ͨChe	ͨChe	Che⁾	Chek ͺ	Screen, this, sugar-cane, a classifier
30	干趕幹割	ͨKon	ͨKon	Kon⁾	Kot ͺ	A shield, to pursue, business, to cut.
31	甘㪺紺蛤	ͨKòm	ͨKòm	Kòm⁾	Kòp ͺ	Sweet, daring, purple, a clam.
32		In these two orders no words occur in				
33		this series				

Second Series, comprising the Lower Tones.

1	2	3	4	Há² ꞏp'ing.	Há² ꞏshŏng.	Há² höü.	Há² yap₂.	Meaning of the Words.
1.	連	璉	鍊	列	ꞏLín	ꞏLín	Lín²	Lít₂	To unite, gem, chain, to separate.
2.	迷	米	袂		ꞏMaí	ꞏMaí	Maí²		To deceive, rice, cuff of the sleeve.
3.	宜	議	貳	熱	ꞏYí	ꞏYí	Yí²	Yít₂	Right, deliberate, the second, hot.
4.	如	語	寓	月	ꞏYü	ꞏYü	Yü²	Yüt₂	As, to converse, to lodge, the moon.
5.	留	柳	陋		ꞏLaú	ꞏLaú	Laú²		To detain, willow, base or mean.
6.	容	勇	用	欲	ꞏYung	ꞏYung	Yung²	Yuk₂	Manner, brave, use, to wish.
7.	靈	領	令	力	ꞏLing	ꞏLing	Ling²	Lik₂	Spiritual, the neck, to order, strength.
8.	文	敏	問	勿	ꞏMan	ꞏMan	Man²	Mat₂	Letters, celerity, to ask, do not.
9.	陽	仰	樣	藥	ꞏYŏng	ꞏYŏng	Yŏng²	Yŏk₂	Light, to look up, pattern, physic.
10.	王	往	旺	鑊	ꞏWong	ꞏWong	Wong²	Wok₂	King, to go, abundance, a pan.
11.	寮	了	料		ꞏLíú	ꞏLíú	Líú²		A window, finished, to estimate.
12.	無	母	務		ꞏMò	ꞏMò	Mò²		Without, mother, business.
13.	元	軟	願	月	ꞏYün	ꞏYün	Yün²	Yüt₂	Origin, flexible, desire, moon.
14.	鞋	蟹	懈		ꞏHaí	ꞏHaí	Haí²		Shoes, crab, lazy.
15.	盟	猛	孟	墨	ꞏMang	ꞏMáng	Máng²	Mak₂	To swear, fierce, first, ink.
16.	詞	似	自		ꞏTs'z	ꞏTs'z	Tsz²		Sentence, like, self.
17.	吟	袵	任	入	ꞏYam	ꞏYam	Yam²	Yap₂	To chant, lappet, to sustain, enter.
18.	茅	卯	貌		ꞏMáú	ꞏMáú	Máú²		Rushes, luxuriant, countenance.
19.	臺	殆	代		ꞏT'oí	ꞏT'oí	Toí²		Terrace, dangerous, instead of.
20.	嚴	染	驗	業	ꞏYím	ꞏYím	Yím²	Yíp₂	Severe, to dye, to examine, occupation.
21.	倫	卵	論	律	ꞏLun	ꞏLun	Lun²	Lut₂	Relation, egg, discourse, law.
22.	雷	蕾	類		ꞏLöü	ꞏLöü	Löü²		Thunder, to involve, species.
23.	鵝	我	臥	岳	ꞏNgo	ꞏNgo	Ngo²	Ngok₂	Goose, I or we, to sleep, certain mountains.
24.	藍	攬	纜	蠟	ꞏLám	ꞏLám	Lám²	Láp₂	Blue, to look, rope, wax.
25.	蘭	懶	爛	辣	ꞏLán	ꞏLán	Lán²	Lát₂	Fading, lazy, broken, pungent.
26.	牙	雅	迓	額	ꞏNgá	ꞏNgá	Ngá²	Ngák₂	Teeth, elegant, to receive, forehead.
27.	門	滿	悶	末	ꞏMún	ꞏMúún	Mún²	Mút₂	Door, full, grief, the end.
28.	梅	每	昧		ꞏMúí	ꞏMúí	Múí²		Plum, each, obscure.
29.	蛇	社	射	石	ꞏShe	ꞏShe	She²	Shek₂	Snake, local deities, to shoot, stone.
30.	寒	旱	翰	褐	ꞏHon	ꞏHon	Hon²	Hot₂	Cold, drought, pencil, hempen cloth.
31.	含	頷	憾	合	ꞏHòm	ꞏHòm	Hòm²	Hòp₂	To endure, jaws, indignation, to unite.
32.	彭	棒	硬	額	ꞏP'áng	ꞏP'áng	Ngáng²	Ngák₂	Abundant, a mace, stiff, forehead.
33.	吾	五	悟		ꞏNg	ꞏNg	Ng²		My or our, five, to perceive.

Tonic Exercise in the 平 ₍P'ing Tones.

1　2　3	Shŏng[2] ₍P'ing ₍P'ín Yam, Shŏng[2] ₍P'ing, and Há[2] ₍P'ing	Meaning of the Words.
1. 瘡办床	₀Ch'ong ₍Ch'ong ₍Ch'ong	Tetter[1], to wound, bed.
2. 香郷揚	₀Hŏng ₍Hŏng ₍Yŏng	Clove[2], a village, to splash.
3. 燶空農	₀Nung ₍Hung ₍Nung	To scorch, empty, to cultivate the ground.
4. 假加	₀Ká ₍Ká	False[3], to add.
5. 膏高蠔	₀Kò ₍Kò ₍Hò	A plaster[4], high, an oyster.
6. 欄蹣攔	₀Lán ₍Lán ₍Lán	A market, to crawl, to prevent.
7. 貓踱茅	₀Máú ₍Maú ₍Máú	A cat, to squat down, reeds.
8. 詩尸匙	₀Shí ₍Shí ₍Shí	A hymn, a corpse, a spoon.
9. 星猩形	₀Sing ₍Sing ₍Ying	A star, an ape, form.
10. 疔丁庭	₀Teng† ₍Teng† ₍T'ing	A tetter sore[1], a nail, a court.
11. 廳聽亭	₀T'eng† ₍T'eng† ₍T'ing	A court[5], to hear, a road-side inn.
12. 丁仃停	₀Ting ₍Ting ₍T'ing	Clove[2], alone, to cease.
13. 打丁婷	₀Ting ₍Ting ₍T'ing	Jingling, a nail, handsome.
14. 璫當堂	₀Tong ₍Tong ₍T'ong	A hawker's hand-gong[6], proper, a hall.
15. 箋煎鐥	₀Tsín ₍Tsín ₍Tsín	Note-paper[7], to fry, a surname.
16. 青清刑	₀Ts'ing ₍Ts'ing ₍Ying	The colour of nature, pure, legal punishments.
17. 艙倉藏	₀Ts'ong ₍Ts'ong ₍Ts'ong	A hold, a granary, to store away.
18. 鎗槍牆	₀Ts'ŏng ₍Ts'ŏng ₍Ts'ŏng	A gun, a spear, a wall.
19. 資貲祠	₀Tsz ₍Tsz ₍T'sz	Postage[8], wealth, spring sacrifice.
20. 意依兒	₀Yí ₍Yí ₍Yí	Will[3], depend on, an infant.
21. 鷹英迎	₀Ying ₍Ying ₍Ying	The hawk, superior, to receive a guest.
22. 英應仍	₀Ying ₍Ying ₍Ying	A salad, suitable, according to.

Other examples might be given, but these will be sufficient for giving the learner a knowledge of these tones.

1. In 火疔瘡 ᶜfo ₀teng ₀ch'ong, tetter.

2. In 丁香 ₀ting ₀hŏng, cloves.

3. As in the phrase 詐假意 chá⁾ ₍ká ₀yí. This phrase is also pronounced chá⁾ ᶜká yí⁾, and also chá⁾ ᶜka ₀yí.

4. In 白蠟膏 pák₂ láp₂ ₀kò, a certain kind of plaster.

5. In 官廳 ₍kwún ₀téng, a court, and in other connections.

6. In 打璫 ₀ting ₀tong, a hawker's hand-gong.

7. In several phrases, the names of different kinds of paper.

8. In 信資 sun⁾ ₍tsz, postage, and in other connections.

Tonic Exercise in the 上 Shŏng² Tones.

	1	2	Shŏng² ᶜshŏng.	Há² ᶜshŏng.	Meaning of the Words.
1.	毆	篓	ᶜAú	ᶜLaú	To fight, a bamboo hamper.
2.	粉	忿	ᶜFan	ᶜFan	Flour of any grain, anger.
3	訪	朗	ᶜLong	ᶜLong	To inquire, lustrous.
4	虎	婦	ᶜFú	ᶜFú	A tiger, lady.
5	喺	蟹	ᶜHaí	ᶜHáí	To be at, a crab.
6.	解	械	ᶜKáí	ᶜK·áí	To explain, to pass anything along.
7.	紀	企	ᶜKéí	ᶜK·éí	Annals, to stand.
8.	矯	臼	ᶜKíú	ᶜKíú	Straight, to bale water.
9.	舉	佢	ᶜKöü	ᶜK·öü	To elevate, he or she.
10.	寡	姆	ᶜKwá	ᶜNá	Widow, used to denote the female.
11.	果	我	ᶜKwo	ᶜNgo	Fruit, I.
12.	叫	禮	ᶜLaí	ᶜLaí	To turn, propriety.
13.	欖	攬	ᶜLám	ᶜLám	Olive, to grasp.
14.	佬	老	ᶜLò	ᶜLò	A fellow, old.
15.	両	兩	ᶜLöng	ᶜLöng	Tael, two.
16.	靄	殆	ᶜOí	ᶜT·oí	Foggy, dangerous.
17.	稟	眼	ᶜPan	ᶜNgán	To petition, eye.
18.	俾	里	ᶜPéí	ᶜLéí	To give, a mile.
19.	表	了	ᶜPíú	ᶜLíú	To manifest, finished.
20.	保	抱	ᶜPò	ᶜP·ò	To protect, to carry in the arms.
21.	使	舓	ᶜShaí	ᶜSháí	To use, to lick.
22.	歹	舵	ᶜTáí	ᶜT·áí	Bad, rudder.
23.	點	斂	ᶜTím	ᶜLím	A dot, to harvest.
24.	頂	挺	ᶜTing	ᶜT·ing	Summit, to pull up.
25.	仔	鱗	ᶜTsaí	ᶜTs·aí	Son, a mullet.
26.	子	似	ᶜTsz	ᶜTs·z	A son, similar.
27.	揾	尹	ᶜWan	ᶜWan	To look for, correct.
28.	碗	滿	ᶜWún	ᶜMúún	A bowl, full.
29.	隠	引	ᶜYan	ᶜYan	Small, to entice.
30.	朽	有	ᶜYaú	ᶜYaú	Rotten wood, to have.
31.	倚	耳	ᶜYí	ᶜYí	To rely on, ear.
32.	掩	染	ᶜYím	ᶜYím	To close, to dye.
33.	夭	擾	ᶜYíú	ᶜYíú	Shortlived, to give trouble.
34.	抉	養	ᶜYöng	ᶜYöng	To shake (as a cloth), to rear.
35.	湧	勇	ᶜYung	ᶜYung	Bubbling, brave.
36.	婉	遠	ᶜYün	ᶜYün	Yielding, distant.

The list of *yap* tones should be studied in the same way as the preceding Exercise.

Tonic Exercise in the Three 入 Yap₂ Tones.

1 2 3	Shŏng² yap₂	Chung yap₂	Há² yap₂	Meaning of the Words.
1. 握鈪嘫	Ak,	Ák.	Ngák₂	To grasp, a bangle, contrary to.
2. 洽鴨陜	Ap,	Áp.	Háp₂	To soak, a duck, a straight passage.
3. 扎壓核	At,	Át.	Hat₂	To thrust in, to press down, the kernel of fruits.
4. 舴責宅	Chák,	Chák.	Chák₂	A small boat, to reprove, a mansion.
5. 執劄閘	Chap,	Cháp.	Cháp₂	To pick up, to write out, a barrier.
6. 郅扎窒	Chat,	Chát.	Chat₂	To ascend, a bundle, to stop up the mouth of.
7. 職隻直	Chik,	Chek,	Chik₂	To govern, one of a pair, straightforward.
8. 竹捉濁	Chuk,	Chuk.	Chuk₂	Bamboo, to seize, turbid.
9. 撮法罰	Fat,	Fát.	Fat₂	To dip up, law, to punish.
10. 急甲及	Kap,	Káp.	K'ap₂	Hasty, coat of mail, and.
11. 骨刮掘	Kwat,	Kwát.	Kwat₂	Bone, to scrape, to dig.
12. 扐肋肋	Lak,	Lák.	Lak₂	To bind, the ribs, the ribs.
13. 笠拹蠟	Lap,	Láp.	Láp₂	A hamper, to lump, wax.
14. 嗶劣律	Lut,	Lüt.	Lut₂	Out of order, infirm, a statute.
15. 乜抹襪	Mat,	Mát.	Mat₂	What? to wipe, stockings.
16. 楲咽皋	Mít,	Yít.	Yít₂	To break off, to choke, the judge or ruler of a city.
17. 燃鈉捺	Nat,	Nát.	Nát₂	Joyful, to smooth, a dash to the right in writing.
18. 吸喢揋	Ngap,	Ngap.	Ngap₂	To talk at random, to tuck in, to beckon.
19. 北百白	Pak,	Pák.	Pák₂	North, hundred, white.
20. 不八魃	Pat,	Pát.	Pát₂	Not, eight, the god of draught.
21. 必鷩別	Pít,	Pít.	Pít₂	Must, a species of pheasant, to separate.
22. 亳榑薄	Pok,	Pok.	P'ok₂	Name of a District, spacious, jungle.
23. 濕恰十	Shap,	Sháp.	Shap₂	Wet, to boil, ten.
24. 失殺實	Shat,	Shát.	Shat₂	To lose, to behead, firm.
25. 恤雪月	Sut,	Süt.	Yüt₂	To compassionate, snow, the moon or a month.
26. 嗒答踏	Tap,	Táp.	Táp₂	To lick, to answer, to step on.
27. 呾笪凸	Tat,	Tát.	Tat₂	Dab, a spot, projecting.
28. 的踢敵	Tik,	T'ek,	Tik₂	Clear, to kick, an opponent.
29. 琢脚署	Tŏk,	Kŏk.	Lŏk₂	To pound on wood, the foot, a little.
30. 則册賊	Tsak,	Ch'ák.	Ts'ák₂	Precept, a register, a thief.
31. 嗻插雜	Tsap,	Ch'áp.	Tsáp₂	A heap, to insert, mixed.
32. 七擦甴	Ts'at,	Ts'át,	Tsát₂	Seven, to brush, a cockroach, as:— 由甲 [kát₂ tsát₂.
33. 卽瘠蓆	Tsik,	Tsik.	Tsek₂†	Immediately, lean, mat.
34. 屈挖滑	Wat,	Wát.	Wát₂	Bent, to scoop out, smooth.
35. 饐醃葉	Yíp,	Yíp.	Yíp₂	Provision for journeys, to salt flesh (to put into brine), a leaf.

Tonic Exercise in the Variant Rising Tones. ✓

	Há² ͵Pʻing Variant.	Shöng² ˢShöng Variant.	Há² ˢShöng Variant.	Shöng² höü³ and ͵Chung yap₂ Variants.	Há² höü³ and Há² yap₂ Variants.	Meanings.
1 嚟	͵Laí					Come,
2 洗		ˢSaí				wash,
1. 3 買			ˢMaí			buy,
4 去 & 跌				Höü³ & tít₀¹		go, fall,
5 問 & 食					Man⁵ & shik₅	ask, eat.
1 抬	͵Tʻoí					Carry,
2 寫		ˢSe				write,
2. 3 冇			ˢMo			none,
4 過 & 抹				Kwo³ & mát₀¹		cross, wipe.
5 賣 & 讀					Maí⁵ & tuk₅	buy, read.
1 行	͵Háng					Walk,
2 走		ˢTsaú				run,
3. 3 上			ˢShöng			go up,
4 閂 & 摺				Fan³ & chip₀¹		sleep, to fold,
5 念 & 學					Ním⁵ & hok₅	to recite, to learn.

Remember that all the variant tones except those of the Upper Even, 上平, shöng² ͵pʻing, and Upper Entering, 上入, shöng² yap₂ are rising tones, that of the Lower Even, 下平, há² ͵pʻing, having first a fall, followed by a rise.

The Upper Rising, 上上, shöng² ˢshöng has a rest at the end of its rise. The Lower Rising, 下上, há² ˢshöng is pronounced with more emphasis, etc. (but see description above), than is bestowed on the variants of the Lower Retiring, 下去, há² höü³, and the Lower Entering, 下入, há² yap₂. Then again the variants of the Upper Retiring 上去, shöng² höü³ and the Middle Entering, 中入, ͵chung yap₂ are both shorter in duration than the others. The variant of the Upper Entering, 上入, shöng² yap₂, is a prolongation of the voice on the same level.

Aspirated and Non-Aspirated Words.

Another distinction which calls for the special attention of the learner is the difference between aspirated and non-aspirated words. ʻIt is a very important part of pronunciation, as much so in every respect as the tones, and should be particularly attended to.ʼ—WILLIAMS's *Easy Lessons in Chinese*, p. 55. ʻIt cannot * * be too strongly impressed upon learners from the outset that * * aspirates * * are of the utmost importance to one who would learn Chinese intelligibly. Carelessness about the difference between aspirated and unaspirated words in Chinese, will often render a speaker as absolutely unintelligible in China, as a foreigner in England would be if he should substitute *d* for *t* or *t* for *d*, saying for instance, " too dry " for " do try," or if he should substitute *b* for *p* or *p* for *b*, speaking of " bears " when he means " pears " and of " pears " when he means " bears. " It is not intended here to assert that the difference between aspirated and unaspirated words is exactly the same as the difference between the English *d* and *t* or *b* and *p* sounds, etc., but the difference is *quite as distinct and great* as this, and it is even more important in speaking Chinese to observe these differences than it is in speaking English.'—FOSTER's *Elementary Lessons in Chinese*, pp. 29 and 30. And yet it is one of the features of Chinese pronunciation which is, one might almost say, systematically ignored by many foreigners learning Chinese, either from a failure to see the distinction, from not understanding the definitions explaining the difference, or from an idea that it can be of no importance. This last idea being probably fostered by the feeling that there is nothing of the kind in English, or in other words, instead of the voice passing quietly from the initial consonant to the vowel and the final consonant, a strong breathing out often takes place in English immediately after the initial consonant. To explain the difference between the aspirated and unaspirated pronunciation let us take, for example, the word ₍tin. To pronounce this word the following actions take place. First place the tip of the tongue on the palate immediately behind the front teeth, then let it quietly drop while the voice pronounces a something between an English *t* and an English *d*, that is, it has the sound of the English *t* but unaccompanied with any forcible emission of the voice, which generally does accompany the pronunciation of the *t* in English, then after this initial consonant immediately follows the *in* pronounced like *een* in English. Next take an aspirated word spelled in the same way, but with an inverted comma to represent the aspirate in Chinese, as:—*t'in*. Here begin as before by placing the tip of the tongue on the palate behind the front teeth, but immediately the tongue falls and the *t* is pronounced, it is followed by a strong breathing out of the voice, this being the way in which many pronounce the *t* in English. There is, however, some difference amongst different speakers of English as to the way in which they pronounce their consonants: that is to say that there is a dual method of pronouncing two precisely similar combinations of letters of the alphabet by different individuals in English, some pronouncing them with a more forcible emission of voice, while others let them, as it were, simply fall quietly out of their mouths without any or but slight propulsion. It therefore follows that the usual directions given as to the pronunciation of the aspirated and unaspirated consonants as pronounced in Chinese are misleading to many persons. To many the directions should be given to pronounce the aspirated consonants in the same way that they do these consonants in English while the unaspirated ones are to be pronounced flatter and more like the other consonants, such as *d* and *b*, which they pronounce without any explosive force of the voice in English.

Now in Chinese certain consonants are pronounced much softer and without any explodent force, while the same consonants are also pronounced in other words with a strong out-breathing of the voice immediately after them, as stated above—suppose, in fact, that a Greek rough breathing comes in ; in other words the consonants in Chinese which are pronounced quietly are also pronounced with a forcible emission of the voice immediately following them which is represented by the inverted comma in the spelling used to show the sound in English of Cantonese. Thus ₍chá, the ch being pronounced quietly means, *to hold*, while the same sound, but intensified by an explosive force, as, ₍ch'á means, *fork*. Just as in English there are two ways of pronouncing the *th* (as for example, *thy* and *thigh*, where the only difference in the sound of the two words consists in the difference between the pronunciation of the *th*); so in Chinese the same English consonants (employed to spell the Chinese) in many cases are used in two different ways, one unaspirated and the other followed by the aspirate.

The consonants which have the aspirate after them are the following, viz. :—

Ch, k, p, t, and ts.

The learner will find it a good practice to go through the following exercise daily at first, till he finds no difficulty at all with the unaspirated and aspirated words :—

渣差 ₍chá, *refuse* ; ₍ch'á, *error*.
齋差 ₍cháí, ('tá ₍cháí, *mass*); ₍ch'áí, *police*.
仄測 chak₎, *slanting* ; ch'ák₀, *to fathom*.
責册 chák₀, *to reprove* ; ch'ák₀, *a register*.
針沈 ₍cham, *a needle* ; ₍ch'am, *to sink*.
斬杉 ʿchám, *to chop off* ; ch'ám₎, *fine*.
眞塵 ₍chan, *true* ; ₍ch'an, *dust*.
盞產 ʿchán, (₍tang ʿchán, *a lamp saucer*); ʿch'án, *to produce*.
睜撐 ₍cháng, *heel* ; ₍ch'áng, *to pole*.
閘插 cháp₂, *a gate* ; ch'áp₀, *to insert*.
扎察 chát₀, *a bundle* ; ch'át₀, *to examine*.
州臭 ₍chaú, *a district* ; ch'aú', *a bad smell*.
爪炒 ʿchaú, *claws* ; ʿch'aú, *to fry in fat*.

遮車 ₍che, *an umbrella* ; ʿch'e, *a carriage*.
隻尺 chek₀ (a Classifier) ; ch'ek₀, *a foot*.
知遲 ₍chí, *to know* ; ₍ch'í, *late*.
占詔 ₍chím, *to divine* ; ʿch'ím, *to flatter* (book).
甐躔 ₍chín, *felt* ; ₍ch'ín, *to tread* (book).
正稱 ₍ching, *the first* ; ₍ch'ing, *to style*.
折設 chít₀, *to snap in two* ; ch'ít₀, *to establish*.
朝朝 ₍chíú, *morning* ; ₍ch'íú, *the Court*.
阻初 ʿcho, *to hinder* ; ₍ch'o, *the beginning*.
着綽 chók₀, *right* ; ch'ók₀, *loose*.
章窓 ₍chöng, *a chapter* ; ₍ch'öng, *a window*.[1]
壯瘡 chong', *robust* ; ₍ch'ong, *a boil*.
豬柱 ₍chü, *a pig*[2] ; ʿch'ü, *a pillar*.
追吹 ₍chöü, *to pursue* ; ₍ch'öü, *to blow*.

1. Or in many connections ₍ch'öng.　　2. Or in many connections ₍chü.

畜竹 chuk, *bamboo*; ch'uk, *domestic animals.*	班裏 pan, *a petition*; p'an, *poor.*
春川 chun, *to allow*; ch'un, *spring.*	攀貧 pán, *a grade*; p'án, *to drag.*
准磚 chūn, *a brick*; ch'ūn, *a hill spring.*	崩朋 pang, *a fracture*; p'ang, *a friend.*
中 chung, *middle*; ch'ung, *to fill*	嘩彭 páng², *bang!*; p'áng, *a land-crab.*
出 chut, *to blame* (book); ch'ut, *to go out.*	不疋 pat, *not*; p'at, *a piece* (of cloth).
鷄溪 kaí, *a fowl*; k'aí, *a clear hill stream.*	包抛 paú, *to wrap up*; p'aú, *to cast* (anchor).
街楷 káí, *a street*; k'áí, *a pattern* (book).	俾皮 péí, *to give*; p'éí, *leather, or skin.*
金斂 kam, *gold*; k'am, *a coverlet*	迫擗 pik, *to urge*; p'ek †, *to throw away*
根芹 kan, *roots*; k'an, *parsley.*	邊片 pín, *the side*; p'ín³, *slip* (slice).
挭羹 kang, *soup*; k'ang², *to oppress.*	兵平 ping, *a soldier*; p'ing, *even.*
急吸 kap, *hasty*; k'ap, *to inhale.*	必撇 pít, *must*; p'ít, *a down stroke.*
吉咳 kat, *lucky*; k'at, *to cough.*	標漂 píú, *a banner*; p'íú, *to bleach.*
鳩掴 kaú, *a pigeon*; k'aú, *to mix.*	波鋪 po, *a wave*; p'o, *a classifier of trees*, etc
交靠 káú, *to unite*; k'aú², *to rely on*	煲摸 pò, *to boil*; p'ò, *to spread out.*
幾棊 kéí, *a few*; k'éí, *chess.*	博勞 pok, *intelligent*; p'ok, *to flap.*
極屐 kik, *very*; k'ek †, *clogs.*	幫旁 pong, *to help*; p'ong, *side.*
兼鉗 kím, *moreover*; k'ím, *tongs.*	杯賠 púí, *a cup*; p'úí, *to indemnify.*
堅掔 kín, *firm*; k'ín, *to lift up* (a cover).	搫盤 pún, *to remove*; p'ún, *a basin.*
京鯨 king, *capital city*; k'ing, *a whale*	蓬 pung², *to run against*; p'ung, *a sail.*
深揭 kít, *clear*; k'ít, *to borrow.*	鉢潑 pút, *a coarse dish*; p'út, *to dash water.*
轎橋 kíú³, *a sedan*; k'íú, *a bridge.*	打他 tá, *to strike*; t'á, *another*
改蓋 koí, *to change*; k'oí³, *a cover.*	低梯 taí, *to bend down*; t'aí, *a ladder.*
各確 kok, *each*; k'ok, *really.*	帶太 táí, *a girdle*; t'áí, *excessive.*
脚却 kōk, *foot*; k'ōk, *to stop* (book).	泵氹 tam, *to hammer*; t'am, *a cess-pool.*
剛匠 kong, *just*; k'ong³, *a sofa.*	擔貪 tám, *to carry*; t'ám, *to covet.*
薑強 kōng, *ginger*; k'ōng, *by force.*	墩吞 tan, *a heap*; t'an, *to swallow.*
居渠 kōū, *to dwell*; k'ōū, *a drain.*	單攤 tán, *alone*; t'án, *to spread open.*
捐拳 kūn, *to squeeze through*; k'ūn, *the fist.*	燈藤 tang, *a lamp*; t'ang, *rattan.*
公窮 kung, *public*; k'ung, *poor.*	答塔 táp, *to answer*; t'áp, *a pagoda.*
缺括 kūt, *deficient*; k'wút, *united strength.*	達撻 tát, *to pervade*; t'át, *a dead loss.*
瓜誇 kwá, *a melon*; k'wá, *to brag.*	斗偷 taú, *a dry measure*; t'aú, *to steal.*
歸規 kwaí, *home*; k'waí, *a custom.*	糴踢 tek †, *to buy rice*; t'ek †, *to kick.*
君裙 kwan, *ruler*; k'wan, *a skirt.*	釘艇 teng †, *a nail*; t'eng †, *a boat.*
光狂 kwong, *light*; k'wong, *mad.*	的剔 tik, *clear*; t'ik, *to scrape off.*
把琶 pá, *to seize*; p'á, *a guitar.*	點添 tím, *a spot*; t'ím, *to increase.*
跛批 paí, *lame*; p'aí, *to pare.*	癲天 tín, *crazy*; t'ín, *the sky.*
擺牌 páí, *to spread out*; p'áí, *a shield.*	玎亭 ting, *a jingling sound*; t'ing, *a pavilion.*
百柏 pák, *hundred*; p'ák, *to clap.*	碟帖 típ², *a plate*; t'íp, *a card.*

鐵跌 tít, to fall; t'ít, iron.	節切 tsít, averse; ts'ít, to cut (in slices)
丟條 tíú, to throw away; t'íú, a classifier.	椒樵 tsíú, pepper; ts'íú, scattered wood.
多拖 to, many; t'o, to lead (by the hand).	左錯 tso, the left; ts'o, wrong.
刀桃 tò, a knife; t'ò, or t'ò, peach.	租粗 tsò, rent; ts'ò, coarse.
代檯 toí², a generation; t'oí, a table.	再哎 tsoí, again; ts'oí! pshaw!
度托 tok, to measure; t'ok, to carry.	作錯 tsok, to make; ts'ok, to tattoo.
當湯 tong, proper; t'ong, soup.	葬倉 tsong, to bury; ts'ong, a granary.
劑妻 tsaí, a dose; ts'aí, a wife.	將鎗 tsöng, shall; ts'öng, a gun.
浸尋 tsam, to soak; ts'am, to look for.	聚取 tsöü², to assemble; ts'öü, to take.
簪蠶 tsám, a hairpin; ts'ám, a silkworm.	足速 tsuk, the foot; ts'uk, hurried.
讚餐 tsán, to praise; ts'án, a meal.	樽巡 tsun, a bottle; ts'un, to cruise.
憎層 tsang, to hate; ts'ang, a layer, or storey.	尊村 tsün, honourable; ts'ün, a village.
噆緝 tsap, handful; ts'ap, to join.	棕松 tsung, coir; ts'ung, the pine tree.
疾七 tsat, disease; ts'at, seven.	絕撮 tsüt, to sunder; ts'üt, a pinch.
走秋 tsaú, to run; ts'aú, autumn.	子慈 tsz, a son; ts'z, mercy.
姐邪 tse, an elder sister; ts'e, depraved.	堆推 töü, a heap; t'öü, to push away.
迹戚 tsik, a foot-mark; ts'ik, related to.	督禿 tuk, to lead; t'uk, a Buddhist priest.
尖簽 tsím, sharp; ts'ím, to subscribe.	敦湍 tun, angry; t'un, a rapid current.
煎千 tsín, to fry; ts'ín, a thousand.	短團 tün, short; t'ün, a globular mass.
晶清 tsing, crystal; ts'ing, pure.	東通 tung, east; t'ung, to go through.
接妾 tsíp, to receive; ts'íp, a concubine.	奪脫 tüt, to take by force; t'üt, to strip.

Long and Short Vowels.

Another most important feature in Cantonese is the long and short vowels and diphthongs. The beginner must drill himself in these daily, and make sure that he is pronouncing a word containing a long vowel with the vowel long and one with a short vowel with the vowel short. Dr. Eitel rightly says about these:— 'Another characteristic feature of the Cantonese dialect is the distinction of long and short vowels and diphthongs, which should be specially studied from the beginning, to accustom the ear to the discrimination of these shades, which is indispensable for a ready and correct understanding of the spoken language.'—Introduction to *Cantonese Dictionary*, p. xiii.

To enable the learner to 'specially study' these distinctions, tables of many of them are here appended; and the learner should go through them with his teacher day by day till perfect, and even then a run through them occasionally will do him good.

握搯鶯洽抗仄針眞筆執質分拂黑痕鏗哈喉金根羮急君幕骨林吟笠用麥蚊盟乜腍鈪菡覂鴨押賣斬盞爭闌扎凡法客閒行呷巧監間廵甲關迸刮鹽冷立辣肇攬盲抹男

ak, to grasp; ák, a bangle.	
am, to cover; ʿám, an unopened flower.	
ang, the nightingale; ang, a jar	
ap, to cover over; áp, a duck.	
at, to thrust in; át, to pawn for a time.	
chak, slanting; chák, to reprove.	
cham, a needle; chám, to cut in two.	
chan true; chán, a shallow cup for oil.	
chang, a harpsichord; cháng, to wrangle.	
chap, to pick up; cháp, a barrier	
chat, substance; chát, a bundle	
fan, to divide; fán, all.	
fat, to brush away; fát, usage.	
hak, black; hák, a guest.	
han, a mark; hán, leisure.	
hang, to knock against; háng, to walk.	
hap, sleepy; háp, to gulp.	
haú, the throat; haú, skilful.	
kam, metal; kám, a gaol.	
kan, root; kán, an interval.	
kang, a thick soup; káng, a by-path.	
kap, hasty; káp, armour for the body.	
kwan, the prince; kwán, to bar a door.	
kwang, rumbling; kwáng, to ramble.	
kwat, bone; kwát, to scrape.	
lam, a grove; lám, a basket.	
lang, a jingle; láng, cold.	
lap, a pottle; láp, to establish.	
lat, to let go; lát, pungent.	
mak, wheat; mák, to break in two.	
man, mosquito; mán, to pull.	
mang, an alliance; máng, blind.	
mat, what; mát, to wipe.	
nam, mellow; nám, male.	

撚粒趌阽啥銀吸抝北貧崩不心新嗰膝深身生濕失泵墩搭凸餉浸親噈七雲核難衲鈉額嚴眼峽齧百攀嘩八三散颯撒衫山嘴恰殺擔單荅達賊簪餐雜擦還滑

nan, to handle; nán, difficult.	
nap, a grain; náp, or náp, quilted	
nat, joyful; nát, to smooth.	
ngak, to swindle; ngák, front	
ngam, foolish; ngám, precipice.	
ngan, money; ngán, eye.	
ngap, to talk wildly; ngáp, to tuck in.	
ngat, to sway; ngát, a rank smell.	
pak, north; pák, one hundred.	
p'an, poor; p'án, to lead.	
pang, an emperor's death; páng, bang!	
pat, not; pát, eight.	
sam, the heart; sám, three.	
san, new; sán, to scatter.	
sap, to enter the mouth; sáp, suddenly	
sat, the knee; sát, to disperse.	
sham, deep; shám, clothes.	
shan, body; shán, mountain.	
shang, to produce; sháng, to scour.	
shap, wet; sháp, to provoke.	
shat, to lose; shát, to kill.	
tam, to pound; tám, to carry from a pole	
tan, a heap; tán, single.	
tap, to be rained on; táp, to answer.	
tat, a tenon; tát, intelligent.	
tsak, bream; ts'ák, a thief.	
tsam, to soak; tsám, hairpin.	
ts'an, related to; ts'án, a meal.	
tsap, a handful; tsáp, mixed.	
ts'at, seven; ts'át, to brush.	
wan, cloud; wán, to return.	
wat, the stony seeds of fruit; wát, smooth.	

The Long and Short Diphthongs aí and áí.

喉挨 ₍aí, *whew!* ₍áí, *to lean upon.*
橋齋 ₍chaí, *to place;* ₍cháí, *to abstain.*
費快 faí², *to spend;* fáí², *quick.*
鷄街 ₍kaí, *a fowl;* ₍káí, *a street.*
歸乖 ₍kwaí, *home;* ₍kwáí, *good* (as a child).
嚟拉 ₍laí, *to come;* ₍láí, *to pull.*
迷埋 ₍maí, *to deceive;* ₍máí, *to hide away.*

篩曬 ₍shaí, *sieve;* sháí², *to dry in the sun.*
低帶 ₍taí, *to bend down;* táí², *a ribbon.*
威壞 ₍waí, *dignity;* wáí², *to spoil.*
泥奶 ₍naí, *clay;* ₍náí, *lady.*
嘅涯 ₍ngaí, *to importune;* ₍ngáí, *beach.*
跛拜 ₍paí, *lame;* páí², *to worship.*

Exercises on the Long and Short Diphthongs aí eí áí.

1. 肺非塊 faí², *the lungs;* ₍feí, *not;* faí², *a lump.*
2. 係禧鞋 haí², *to be;* ₍heí, *happy;* ₍háí, *a shoe.*
3. 髻幾街 ᶜkaí, *coiffure;* ᶜkeí, *subtle;* ₍káí, *a street.*
4. 嚟李拉 ₍laí, *to come;* ᶜleí, *a plum;* ₍láí, *to pull.*
5. 米微賣 ᶜmaí, *rice;* ₍meí, *minute;* máí², *to sell.*
6. 塊你乃 ₍naí, *mire;* ᶜneí, *you;* ᶜnáí, *but.*
7. 矗俾擺 paí², *sad;* ᶜpeí, *to give;* ᶜpáí, *to spread out.*
8. 弟地大 taí², *a younger brother;* téí², *earth;* táí², *great.*

The Long and Short Diphthongs aú and áú.

區拗 ₍aú, *a surname;* ᶜáú, *to snap in two.*
周找 ₍chaú, *universal;* ᶜcháú, *to exchange*
喉巧 ₍haú, *the throat;* ᶜháú, *skilful.*
九絞 ₍kaú, *nine;* ᶜkáú, *to twist.*
流撈 ₍laú, *to flow;* ₍láú, *to drag for in water.*

蹲茅 ₍maú, *to squat down;* ₍máú, *reeds.*
扭鬧 ₍naú, *to twist;* náú², *to scold.*
牛咬 ₍ngau, *an ox;* ᶜngáú, *to bite.*
剖包 ₍p'aú, *to divide;* ₍páú, *to wrap around.*
收筲 ₍shaú, *to receive;* ₍sháú, *a basket.*

Exercise on e and í (= ee).

車知 ₍ch'e, *a carriage;* ₍chí, *to know.*
唏顯 ₍he! *holloa!* ᶜhín, *manifest.*
嘅見 ke², *sign of possessive;* kín², *to see.*
哩蓮 ₍le, *a final particle;* ₍lín, *the lotus.*
歪面 ₍me, *awry;* mín², *the face.*
喴年 ₍ne, *there!* ₍nín, *year*

喉鳴 ₍nge, *whine;* ₍ngí, *hesitating.*
啤便 ₍pe, *beer;* pín², *convenient.*
寫先 ᶜse, *to write;* ₍sín, *first.*
賒善 ₍she, *on credit;* shín², *virtuous.*
爹天 ₍te, *dad;* ₍t'ín, *the sky.*
借箭 tse², *to borrow;* tsín², *an arrow.*

Exercise on Short and Long I, viz., I and í.

織知 chik, *to weave*; chí, *to know*.
搖顯 fing², *to swing*; hín, *manifest*.
京潔 king, *a capital*; kit, *pure*.
隙唎 kwik, *a crack*; kwít, *shrill*.
齡憐 ling, *tinkling*; lín, *commiserate*.
明勉 ming, *clear*; mín, *to force*.
擰脔 ning, *to take*; nín, *a slice*.

兵變 ping, *a soldier*; pín, *to alter*.
星仙 sing, *a star*; sín, *genii*.
聲詩 shing, *a sound*; shí, *a hymn*.
定典 ting², *to fix*; tín, *a canon*.
淨煎 tsing², *pure*; tsin, *to fry*.
标擰 wing, *to throw*; wit, *creaking*.

Whenever o is only used with an initial consonant or consonants and without a final consonant both the open o, and close ò are used in the Cantonese.

Exceptions:—cho, fo, kwo, and wo, there being no chò, fò, kwò, or wò.

Whenever the o is followed by the final consonants k, n, ng, and t, then the o is an open one, as:—ok, on, ong, and kot.

Whenever the o is followed by the final consonant m, and p, then it has the close sound of ò, as òm, kòp.

Exercise on Long and Short o, viz., o and ò.

阻早 cho, *to hinder*; tsò, *early*.
何毫 ho, *what?* hò, *down* (hair).
歌高 ko, *a song*; kò, *high*.
攞佬 lo, *to fetch*; lò, *a fellow*.
磨毛 mo, *to rub*; mò, *hair*.

鵝鏨 ngo, *a goose*; ngò, *to shake*.
波鎅 po, *a wave*; pò, *to boil*.
疎數 sho, *wide apart*; shò², *an account*.
鎖鬚 so, *a lock*; sò, *a beard*.
左做 tso, *left*; tsò², *to do*.

There are other combinations in which the o both long and short are used; but in these other combinations only one kind of o is used with each combination; they do not therefore come into such striking contrast as when appearing simply with initial consonants, and, moreover, the above Exercise is sufficient to give the learner a knowledge of the difference between the two pronunciations.

Exercise on u, ú and ü.

准寬尊 chun, *to permit*; fún, *to relax*; chün, *single*.
倫門亂 lun, *constant*; mún, *door*; lün², *confused*.
順本般 shun², *compliant*; pún, *the origin*; shün, *a ship*.

These will be sufficient to show the difference between these sounds.

Exercise on ōü and úí.

追灰   _cchöü, *to pursue ;* _cfúí, *ashes*

水杯   ^cshöü, *water ;* _cpúí, *a cup.*

最囘   tsöü[?], *to assemble;* _cwúí, *a time.*

These few examples will show the difference between these two sounds ; but the learner must note that the English Dictionaries of Cantonese, which are nearly all based on the *Fan Wan*, are not to be trusted for giving these sounds ; some that should be under öü are classed with those under úí, and again others belonging to these classes are spelled with the ü.

The Chinese, not having an alphabetical language and therefore not being accustomed to such a mode of representing the sounds, have not their ears so acutely trained to distinguish between slight distinctions and differences in sounds as represented by letters of the alphabet, as they are to distinguish differences in the tones, and are consequently not altogether to be trusted in their classifications of sounds. Dictionary makers should take the correct pronunciation of good speakers of a standard dialect (such for example as Canton-city Cantonese) instead of blindly following the guidance of native compilations, which sometimes mislead.

————

Pronunciation.

a like u, e g.:- san, *as* sun

á ,, ah, e.g.:—pá, *as* pa

e ,, e in men, e.g.:—meng

i ,, i in pin, e.g.:—king, *as* king.

í ,, í in machine, e.g.:—kín, *as* keen.

o ,, o in order, e.g.:—ho, *as* haw.

ò ,, ò in so, e.g.:—mò, *as* (to) mow.

ö nearly like er in her, e.g.—hö, *as* he(r)

u ,, ,, u in hur, e.g.:—shun.

ú like u in fool, e.g.:—wú, *as* woo.

ü ,, French u in l'une, e.g.:—süt.

aí ,, i in while, e.g.:—faí.

áí like i in high, e.g.:—fáí, *as* fie.

aú ,, ou in plough, e.g.:—haú, *as* how.

áú ,, aaow, e.g.:—háú.

éí ,, ey in they, e.g.:—p'éí, *as* pay.

íú ,, ew in few, e.g.:—shíú.

oí ,, oy in boy, e.g.:—k'oí, *as* coy.

öü nearly as in louis, e g.:—shöü.

úí like ooee, e.g.:—múí.

sz, run the sounds of the letters *s* and *z* together.

m is the sound of the letter m alone without any vowel and formed with the lips closed.

ng like ng in sing.

There is no b, d, g alone, j, q, v, x or z sounds in Cantonese. The nearest approach to r is in the word for *boot*, which sounds very much like *her*, as an Englishman who scarcely pronounces his *r* would sound it, not as a Scotchman would pronounce it.

The rest of the letters are pronounced as in English. The only difficulty the learner will find will be in pronouncing them soft enough when unaspirated (especially is this true with the letters *p*, *k* and *t*), as we generally pronounce those consonants in English, which are sometimes followed by aspirates in Chinese with sufficient force to render them aspirated, though in some parts of England they are always pronounced unaspirated.

Be very careful about the distinction between the short *a* and the long *á*. Men that have lived many years in China are often so oblivious of the living pronunciation as not to notice that they are led away by the peculiar use of this short *a* to represent a *u*—and in fact pronounce San Ning as spelled, and not as Sun Ning, the correct sound. This is a most common mistake with Europeans, and it is extremely disagreeable and pitiable to hear the persistence with which they will adhere to this egregious mistake, for there is no such sound in Chinese as "san" in sandy.

To correct such and similar tendencies a syllabary is here appended in which, whenever possible to do so, the Chinese sounds have been represented by sounds of the English letters, or by words in English, etc.. so that between the list given above and this that follows the learner ought. especially with the assistance of his teacher, to arrive at the correct pronunciation.

Let the learner remember that this is of great importance.

The *sh* in Cantonese is pronounced softer than in English.

SYLLABARY OF CANTONESE.

THE ORTHOGRAPHY ADOPTED IN THIS BOOK REPRESENTED BY SIMILAR SOUNDS IN ENGLISH, ETC., WHEN SUCH SOUNDS EXIST, OR BY COMBINATIONS OF THE LETTERS OF THE ENGLISH ALPHABET.

Only the letters not bracketed are to be imitated in sound, but with the sound that they have when in union with those in brackets.

If blanks are left in the syllabary it is in consequence of no equivalent sounds appearing in English, or under such circumstances it is stated that the sound is nearly, or somewhat like such and such a combination of English letters. In such cases the former list and a careful imitation of the Chinese voice ought to assist the beginner, especially with perseverance, to attain to what at first may seem to him almost to necessitate an impossible contortion of his vocal organs.

Even when tolerably sure of his pronunciation, the beginner will find it of advantage to check it by this syllabary, as mistakes at first generally result in a tendency to a permanently vicious pronunciation, which, when once fixed, will be very difficult to change.

The unaspirated words the learner will notice, by listening to his teacher, are pronounced much softer and without the explodent force which the aspirated words have. The sounds of the consonants when unaspirated must be particularly noticed. They sound much flatter than the English consonants, which are used to represent the nearest approach to their sound. Remember that ch unaspirated is much flatter than ch in English, almost reaching the dj. but never actually that. In order to draw particular attention to this sound of some of the consonants the aspirated ones are followed by an h in the English spelling in this syllabary, though it must be remembered, as said before, that the aspirated consonants often approach nearer to the English sound of the consonants than the unaspirated ones in Chinese.

ch unaspirated sounds almost midway between the English sounds of *dj* and *ch.*

k	,,	,,	,,	,,	*g* ,, *k.*
kw	,,	,,	,,	,,	*gw* ,, *kw.*
p	,,	,,	,,	,,	*b* ,, *p.*
t	,,	,,	,,	,,	*d* ,, *t.*
ts	,,	,,	,,	,,	*ds* ,, *ts.*

These are the only consonants and combinations of consonants which are followed by the aspirate.

There are in Cantonese 780 different syllables or words which are represented by a different spelling in English.

A

Á *as* ah!	Ám *as* a(r)m.	At *as* (h)ut
Aí *as* i(dle)	Án *as* A(h)n(hold).	Át *as* (h)a(r)t.
Áí *as* eye, *or* aye.	Ang *as* (h)ung.	Aú *as* (h)ow.
Ak *as* Ux (bridge) *	Áng *as* ahng.	Aú *as* a(h)oo.
Ák *as* a(r)k.	Ap *as* up	
Am *as* (h)um.	Áp *as* (h)a(r)p	

C

Chá *as* cha(rm).	Ch'ak *as* chhuck.	Chan *as* chun.
Ch'á *as* chha(rm).	Chák *as* chahk	Ch'an *as* chhun.
Chaí *as* chi(ld).	Ch'ák *as* chhahk	Chán *as* chahn.
Cháí *as* Chi(na).	Cham *as* chum	Ch'án *as* chhahn.
Ch'aí *as* Chhi.	Ch'am *as* chhum.	Chang *as* ch(h)ung.†
Ch'áí *as* Chhi(na)	Chám *as* cha(r)m	Cháng *as* chahng.
Chak *as* chuck.	Ch'ám *as* chha(r)m.	Ch'áng *as* chhahng.

* Like Uk, that is to say the s in the x not being sounded.
† Not choong, but the word is pronounced as if the h of hung were changed into ch.

Chap *as* chup.

Cháp *as* chahp

Ch'áp *as* chhahp.

Chat *as* chut(ney).

Chát *as* cháht.

Ch'át *as* chhaht.

Chaú *as* chow.

Ch'aú *as* chhow.

Cháú *as* cha(h)ow.

Ch'áú *as* chha(h)oo.

Che *as* che(rry).

Ch'e *as* chhe(rry).

Chek *as* chek.

Ch'ek *as* chhek.

Cheng *as* cheng.

Ch'et *as* chhet.

Chí *as* cheese.

Ch'í *as* chhee(se)

Chik *as* chick.

Ch'ik *as* chhick.

Chím *as* cheem.

Ch'ím *as* chheem.

Chín *as* cheen.

Ch'ín *as* chheen.

Ching *as* ching.

Ch'ing *as* chhing

Chíp *as* cheep.

Chít *as* cheat.

Ch'ít *as* chhee(tah).

Chíú *as* cheeoo.

Ch'íú *as* chheeoo.

Cho *as* chaw.

Ch'o *as* chhaw

Chok *as* chalk.

Chŏk *as* Ch(h)u(r)k *

Ch'ŏk *as* Chh(h)u(r)k *

Chong *as* chong

Ch'ong *as* chhong

Chŏng *as* Ch(h)u(r)ng. *

Ch'ŏng *as* Chh(h)u(r)ng. *

Chū *as* chue.

Ch'ū *as* chhue

Chŏŭ *something like* chooee.

Ch'ŏŭ *something like* chhooee.

Chuk *something like* chook.

Ch'uk *something like* chhook.

Chun *as* chu(r)n.

Ch'un *as* chhu(r)n.

Chūn *as* chune.

Ch'ūn *as* chhune, *combination of* ch *and French* une.

Chung *as* choong.

Ch'ung *as* chhoong.

Chut *as* ch(h)u(r)t

Ch'ut *somewhat like* chut(ney). but purse the lips together.

Chūt *as* Chuet

E

E *as* e(dible).

F

Fá *as* Fa(ther).

Faí *as* fi(ne).

Fáí *as* fi(delity).

Fák *as* Fa(r)q(uhar).

Fan *as* fun.

Fán *as* fahn.

Fang *as* f(h)ung.

Fat *as* fut.

Fát *as* faht.

Faú *as* fow.

Féí *as* fay.

Fik *as* fick(le)

Fing *as* fing(er).

Fít *as* feet.

Fo *as* fo(rtune).

Fok *as* fok.

Fong *as* fong

Fú *as* foo(l).

Fuí *as* fooee.

Fuk *as* fook

Fún *as* foon.

Fung *as* fung

Fút *as* fŏŏt.

H

Há *as* Ha!

Haí *as* hi(de).

Háí *as* high.

Hak *as* huck(ster).

Hák *as* ha(r)k.

Ham *as* hum

Hám *as* ha(r)m.

Han *as* hun.

Hán *as* hahn.

* This u to be pronounced like the German ŏ.

Hang *as* hung

Háng *as* hahng

Hap *as* hup.

Háp *as* ha(r)p.

Hat *as* hut

Haŭ *as* how.

Háŭ *as* ha(h)ow.

Hé *as* hey.

Héí *as* hay

Hím *as* heem

Hín *as* heen

Hing *as* hing

Híp *as* heep

Hít *as* heat.

Híŭ *as* hew, *or* heeoo

Ho *as* haw

Hò *as* Ho!

Hö *as* he(r)

Hoí *as* (ship a) hoy!

Hok *as* hock

Hòm *something between* ho(r)m *and* hum

Hòn *as* ho(r)n.

Hong *as* hong.

Höng *as* he(r)ng

Hòp *something between* ho(r)p *and* hut.

Hot *as* ho(r)t(iculture

Höü *nearly* hooee

Huk *as* hook.

Hün *as* huen

Hung *as* hung

Hüt *as* huet.

K

Ká *as* ca(r).

K'á *as* khá

Kaí *as* ki(te).

K'aí *as* khi(te).

Káí *as* c(r)y.

K'áí *as* ch(r)y

K'ak *as* k(h)uck.

Kák *as* kahk.

Kam *as* come

K'am *as* chome.

Kám *as* Ca(r)m(el).

Kan *as* kun.

K'an *as* khun.

Kán *as* khan.

Kang *as* k(h)ung.

K'ang *as* khung.

Káng *as* cangue

Kap *as* cup.

K'ap *as* khup.

Káp *as* ca(r)p.

Kat *as* cut.

K'at *as* khut.

Kát *as* ca(r)t.

Kaŭ *as* cow.

K'aŭ *as* khow.

Káŭ *as* ka(h)ow.

K'áŭ *as* kha(h)ow

Ke *as* ca(re)

K'e *as* cha(re)

Kéí *as* kay.

K'éí *as* khay

Kek *as* keck.

K'ek *as* kheck.

K'em *as* k(h)em.

Keng *as* keng.

K'eng *as* kheng.

Kik *as* kick.

K'ik *as* khick.

Kím *as* keem.

K'ím *as* kheem.

Kín *as* keen.

K'ín *as* kheen.

King *as* king.

K'ing *as* khing.

Kíp *as* keep.

Kít *as* keet.

K'ít *as* kheet.

Kíŭ *as* keeoo.

K'íŭ *as* kheeoo

Ko *as* co(r)e

Kò *as* co(de).

Koí *as* coy.

K'oí *as* khoy.

Kok *as* cock

K'ok *as* khock.

Kòm *as* co(r)m

Kòn *as* co(r)n

Kong *as* kong

K'ong *as* khong

Kòp *as* co(r)p(se).

Kot *as* cou(r)t.

Kök *as* ke(r)k.

K'ök *as* khe(r)k

Köng *as* ku(r)ng.

K'öng *as* khu(r)ng

Köü *nearly like* kooee.

K'öü *nearly like* khooee

Kuk *as* cook.

K'uk *as* khook.

Kün *as* kune.*

K'ün *as* khune.

Kung *as* koong.

* This has the sound of the French word une with a k prefixed.

K'ung *as* khoong.

Küt *as* kuet.

K'üt *as* khu(e)t.

Kwá *as* qua(lm)

K'wá *as* qhua(lm)

Kwaí *as* kwiee

K'waí *as* khwiee

Kwáí *as* qui(etus)

K'waí *as* khwai.

Kwák *as* kwahk.

Kwan *as* kwun

K'wan *as* khwun.

Kwán *as* kwahn

Kwang *as* kwung.

Kwáng *as* kwahng.

K'wáng *as* khwang.

Kwat *as* kwut

Kwát *as* kwaht

Kwe *as* kweh.

K'weng *as* khweng.

Kwik *as* quick.

Kwing *as* kwing

Kwít *as* kweet.

Kwo *as* kwoh.

Kwok *as* kwok.

Kwong *as* kwong.

K'wong *as* khwong

Kwú *as* kwoo.

K'wú *as* khwoo.

Kwuí *as* kwooee

Kwún *as* kwoon.

Kwút *as* kwoot.

L

Lá *as* La!

Laí *as* (g)li(de)

Láí *as* lie

Lak *as* luck.

Lák *as* la(r)k.

Lam *as* Lum(ley)

Lám *as* Lahm.

Lan *as* Lun(dy).

Lán *as* lahn.

Lang *as* lung.

Láng *as* lahng

Lap *as* lup.

Láp *as* lahp.

Lat *as* Lut(ton).

Lát *as* laht.

Laú *as* l(h)ow.

Láú *as* la(h)oo.

Le *as* l(th)e(re)

Léí *as* lay.

Leng *as* leng.

Lik *as* lick.

Lím *as* leem.

Lín *as* lean.

Ling *as* ling.

Líp *as* leap

Lít *as* lit(re)

Líú *as* leeoo

Lo *as* law

Lò *as* Lo!

Lö *as* ler *

Loí *as* (al)loy.

Lok *as* lock.

Lom *as* lom.

Long *as* long

Lök *as* le(r)

Löng *as* le(r)ng.

Löü *somewhat like* looee

Luk *as* look.

Lun *as* lea(r)n.

Lün *as* l'une.

Lung *as* lung

Lut *as* l(h)u(r)t.

Lüt *something like* looeet.

M

M *as* m(a).

Má *as* ma.

Maí *as* mi(ne)

Máí *as* my.†

Mak *as* muck.

Mák *as* mahk.

Man *as* mun(dane).

Mán *as* mahn.

Mang *as* mung.

Máng *as* mahng

Mat *as* mut(ter).

Mát *as* maht.

Maú *as* mow.

Máú *as* ma(h)oo.

Me *as* me(ddle).

Meng *as* meng

Méí *as* may.

Mik *as* mick.

Mín *as* mean

Ming *as* ming.

Mít *as* meat.

* Only give the faintest ghost of a sound to the er.

† An open full sound.

Míú *as* mew.	Mok *as* mawk.	Mún *as* moon.
Mo *as* maw.	Mong *as* mong.	Múún *as* mooon.
Mò *as* mo(de).	Múí *as* mooee	Mung *as* moong
Mom *as* mom.	Muk *as* mook.	Mút *as* moot

N

Ná *as* nah.	Ngák *as* (si)ng-ahk	Ni, *or* Ní *as* nih, *or* nee
Naí *as* ni(ne).	Ngam *as* (si)ng-um.	Néí *as* ney
Náí *as* nigh.	Ngám *as* (si)ng-ahm	Nik *as* nick.
Nak *as* nuk.	Ngan *as* (si)ng-un.	Ním *as* neem.
Nam *as* numb.	Ngán *as* (si)ng-ahn.	Nín *as* neen.
Nám *as* nahm.	Ngang *as* (si)ng-ung.	Ning *as* ning
Nan *as* nun.	Ngáng *as* (si)ng-ahng	Níp *as* neap.
Nán *as* nahn.	Ngap *as* (si)ng-up.	Nít *as* neat.
Nang *as* nung	Ngáp *as* (si)ng-ahp	Níú *as* neeoo
Nap *as* nup	Ngat *as* (si)ng-ut.	No *as* no(r)
Náp *as* nahp	Ngát *as* (si)ng-aht.	Nò *as* no.
Nat *as* nut.	Ngaú *as* (si)ng-(h)ow.	Noí *as* (an)noy.
Nát *as* naht.	Ngáú *as* (si)ng-ahow.	Nok *as* knock.
Naú *as* now	Nge *as* (si)ng-(th)e(re)	Nong *as* nong
Náú *as* naaow.	Ngí *as* (si)ng-ee	Nõng *as* nu(rr)ng
Ne *as* Ne(d).	Ngít *as* (si)ng-eat.	Nöü *somewhat like* nooee.
Neng *as* neng.	Ngo *as* (si)ng-awe	Nuk *as* nook.
Ng *as* (si)ng	Ngò *as* (si)ng-oh!	Nün *as* nune.*
Ngá *as* (si)ng-ah!	Ngoí *as* (si)ng-(ah)oi.	Nung *as* noong.
Ngaí *as* (si)ng-i(dle)	Ngok *as* (si)ng-(s)ock.	Nut *as* nu(r)t(ure)
Ngáí *as* (si)ng-eye.	Ngon *as* (si)ng-(h)on(g)	
Ngak *as* (si)ng-uk.	Ngong *as* (si)ng-(h)ong	

O

O *as* awe.	Ok *as* awk(ward)	On *as* o(r)n(ament)
O *as* oh!	Ök *as* euk.	Ong *as* (s)ong.
Oí *as* (h)oy	Òm *as* u(r)m.	

P

Pá *as* pa	P'aí *as* phi(ne)	Pak *as* puck.
P'á *as* pha	Páí *as* pie	Pák *as* pa(r)k
Paí *as* pi(ne)	P'áí *as* phie	P'ák *as* pha(r)k

* French une.

P'an *as* pun.

P'an *as* phun.

P'án *as* pahn

P'án *as* phahn

Pang *as* p(h)ung

P'ang *as* phung *

P'áng *as* pahng.

P'áng *as* phahng

P'at *as* put.

P'at *as* phut.

P'át *as* paht.

Paú *as* pow.

P'aú *as* phow

P'áú *as* pa(h)ow

P'áú *as* pha(h)oo

P'e *as* peh

Péí *as* pay.

P'éí *as* p(h)ay.

Peng *as* peng.

P'eng *as* pheng.

Pik *as* pick

P'ik *as* phick.

Pín *as* peen.

P'ín *as* pheen.

Ping *as* ping

P'ing *as* phing.

Pít *as* peat.

P'ít *as* pheat.

Píú *as* peeoo

P'íú *as* pheeoo.

Po *as* paw.

P'o *as* phaw

Pò *as* Po.

P'ò *as* Pho.

Pok *as* pawk

P'ok *as* phawk.

Pòm *as* pom.

P'òm *as* phom.

Pong *as* pong.

P'ong *as* phong.

Pop *nearly as* Pu(r)p

P'op *nearly as* phu(r)p

Púi *as* pooee

P'úi *as* phooee

Puk *as* pook

P'uk *as* phook.

Pún *as* poon.

P'ún *as* phoon.

Pung *as* poong

P'ung *as* phoong *

Pút *as* put

P'út *as* phoot.

S

Sa *as* sah.

Saí *as* cy(der).

Sáí *as* sigh.

Sak *as* suck

Sam *as* some.

Sám *as* sahm

San *as* sun.

Sán *as* sahn.

Sang *as* sung

Sap *as* sup

Sáp *as* sahp.

Sat *as* sut

Sát *as* saht.

Saú *as* sow.

Sáú *as* saou

Se *as* Se(ttle)

Seng *as* seng.

Shá *as* Shah

Shaí *as* shi(ne)

Sháí *as* shy.

Shák *as* sha(r)k

Sham *as* shum.

Shám *as* shahm.

Shan *as* shun

Shán *as* shahn.

Shang *as* sh(h)ung

Sháng *as* shahng

Shap *as* shup

Sháp *as* sha(r)p

Shat *as* shut

Shát *as* shaht

Shaú *as* shhow.

Sháú *as* sha(h)oo.

Shé *as* sche(dule)

Sheng *as* sheng

Shí *as* she.

Shik *as* shik

Shím *as* sheem.

Shín *as* sheen.

Shing *as* shing

Shíp *as* sheep.

Shít *as* sheet

Shíú *as* sheeoo.

Sho *as* Shaw.

Shò *as* show.

Shok *as* shock.

Shong *as* shong.

Shök *as* shi(r)k.

Shöng *as* she(r)ng.

Shü *as* chu(t).

Shöü *nearly like* shooee.

* That is to say pronounce *hung*, then put a *p* in the place of *h*, retaining the same pronunciation to the rest of the letters as before.

Shuk *as* shook.

Shŭn *as* shune.

Shun *as* shu(r)n.

Shung *as* shoong.

Shut *as* shi(r)t.

Shŭt *nearly* shuet.

Sik *as* sick.

Sín *as* seen.

Sing *as* sing.

Síp *as* s(l)eep.

Sít *as* seat.

Síú *as* seeoo.

So *as* swo(rd).

Sò *as* so.

Sŏ *as* si(r)

Soí *as* soy.

Sok *as* sawk.

Sŏk *as* se(r)k

Song *as* song.

Sŏng *as* su(r)ng.

Söü *nearly like* sooee.

Suk *as* sook.

Sun *as* (con)ce(r)n.

Sŭn *as* sooeene.

Sung *as* soong

Sut *as* (con)ce(r)t.

Sŭt *as* suet; *pronounce the word quickly and run the vowels together.*

Sz *join* s *and* z *and sound together, beginning with a simple* s *and passing on to the sound of the* z.

T

Tá *as* tah

T‘á *as* thah

Taí *as* ti(dy)

T‘aí *as* thi(dy).

Táí *as* tie

T‘áí *as* thie.

Tak *as* tuck.

Tam *as* tum.

T‘am *as* thum.

Tám *as* tahm.

T‘ám *as* thahm.

Tan *as* tun.

T‘an *as* thun.

Tán *as* tahn

T‘án *as* thahn.

Tang *as* tong(ue).

T‘ang *as* thong(ue).

Tap *as* tup.

T‘ap *as* thup.

Táp *as* tahp.

T‘áp *as* thahp.

Tat *as* tut.

Tát *as* taht.

T‘át *as* thaht.

Taú *as* t(h)ow.

T‘aú *as* thhow.

Te *as* tea(r).

Teí *as* t(h)ey.

Teng *as* teng.

T‘eng *as* theng.

Tí, *or* tí *as* tih, *or* tea.

Tik *as* tick.

T‘ik *as* thick.

Tím *as* team.

T‘ím *as* theam

Tín *as* teen.

T‘ín *as* theen.

Ting *as* ting.

T‘ing *as* thing.

Típ *as* teep.

T‘íp *as* theep.

Tít *as* teet.

T‘ít *as* theet.

Tíú *as* teeoo.

T‘íú *as* theeoo.

To *as* to(re).

T‘o *as* Tho(re).

Tò *as* toe.

T‘ò *as* thoe.

Toí *as* toy.

T‘oí *as* thoy.

Tok *as* talk.

T‘ok *as* thalk.

Tŏk *as* te(r)k

Tong *as* Tong(a).

T‘ong *as* Thong(a).

Tò *as* t(h)u(r).

Tŏng *as* te(r)ng.

Tsá *as* tsah.

Tsaí *as* tsie

Ts‘aí *as* tshie.

Ts‘áí *as* tshahi.

Tsak *as* tsuk.

Tsák *as* tshahk.

Tsam *as* tsum.

Ts‘am *as* tshum.

Tsám *as* tsahm.

Ts‘ám *as* tshahm.

Ts‘an *as* tsun.

Tsán *as* tsahn.

Ts‘án *as* tshahn.

Tsang *as* ts(h)ung.

Ts‘ang *as* tshung.

Tsap *as* tsup.

Ts‘ap *as* tshup.

Tsáp *as* tsahp.

Tsat *as* tsut.

Ts‘at *as* tshut.

Tsát *as* tsaht.

Ts'at *as* tshaht.

Tsaú *as* ts(h)ow.

Ts'aú *as* tshow.

Tse *as* ts(th)e(re).

Ts'e *as* tsh(th)e(re).

Tseng *as* tseng.

Ts'eng *as* tsheng.

Tsik *as* tsik.

Ts'ik *as* tshik.

Tsím *as* tseem.

Ts'ím *as* tsheem.

Tsín *as* tseen.

Ts'ín *as* tsheen.

Tsing *as* tsing.

Ts'ing *as* tshing.

Tsíp *as* tseep.

Ts'íp *as* tsheep.

Tsít *as* tseet.

Ts'ít *as* tsheet.

Tsíú *as* tseeoo.

Ts'íú *as* tsheeoo.

Tso *as* tsawe.

Ts'o *as* tshawe.

Tsò *as* tso.

Ts'ò *as* tsho.

Tsoí *as* tsoy.

Ts'oí *as* tshoy.

Tsok *as* tsawk.

Ts'ok *as* tshawk.

Tsong *as* tsawng.

Ts'ong *as* tshawng.

Tsŏng *as* tsu(rr)ng.

Ts'ŏng *as* tshu(rr)ng.

Tsŏü *nearly like* tsooee.

Ts'ŏü *nearly like* tshooee

Tsuk *as* tsook.

Ts'uk *as* tshook.

Tsun *as* tsu(r)n.

Ts'un *as* tshu(r)n.

Tsūn *as* tsooeene.

Ts'ūn *as* tshooeene.

Tsung *as* tsoong,

Ts'ung *as* tshoong

Tsut *as* ts(h)u(r)t.

Tsūt *as* tsooeet.

Ts'ūt *as* tshooeet.

Tsz *as* tsz.

Ts'z *as* tshz.

Tŏü *nearly like* tooee.

T'ŏü *nearly like* thooee

Tu *as* too.

Tuk *as* took

T'uk *as* thook

Tun *as* tu(r)n.

T'un *as* thu(r)n.

Tün *as* *tune.**

T'ün *as* *thune.**

Tung *as* toong.

T'ung *as* thoong.

Tūt *nearly like* tooeet

T'üt *nearly like* thooeet.

U

Uk *something between* uk *and* ook.

Ung *as* ooong.

W

Wá *as* wah.

Waí *as* wei.

Waí *as* Wye.

Wák *as* wahk.

Wan *as* one.

Wán *as* wahn.

Wang *as* wung.

Wáng *as* wahng.

Wat *as* wut.

Wát *as* waht.

We *as* we(ar).

Wí *as* wee.

Wik *as* wick.

Wing *as* wing.

Wít *as* weet.

Wo *as* wa(r)

Wok *as* walk.

Wong *as* wong.

Wú *as* woo.

Wuí *as* wooee.

Wún *as* woon.

Wút *as* woot

Y

Yá *as* yah.

Yaí *as* yi(dle).

Yák *as* yahk.

Yam *as* yum.

Yan *as* yun.

Yáng *as* ya(h)ng.

Yap *as* yup.

Yáp *as* yahp.

Yat *as* yut.

* French une.

Yaú *as* y(h)ow.	Ying *as* ying.	Yúí *as nearly* yooee.
Yáú *as* ya(h)oo.	Yíp *as* yeep	Yuk *as* yook.
Ye *as* ye(ar).	Yít *as* yeet.	Yun *as* yu(r)n.*
Yí *as* ye.	Yíú *as* yeeoo.	Yûn *as* yune.
Yik *as* yik.	Yök *as* yu(r)k.	Yung *as* yoong.
Yím *as* yeem.	Yöng *as* yu(r)ng.*	Yût *as* yueet.
Yín *as* yeen.	Yü *as* yue.	

* It is well nigh impossible to represent the difference between this *ö* and *u*; but it may be of some assistance to know that the former is pronounced with the lips open, while the lips require to be pursed together in pronouncing the latter.

TONIC MARKS
AND
ABBREVIATIONS USED IN THIS BOOK.

[C.] = Classifier.

[S. of p. t.] = Sign of past time.

Lit. = Literally.

* Indicates that the tone the word is marked in is different from the tone in the book language, and generally that it is one of the variant rising-tones

† Indicates that the pronunciation of the word as given in this book is different from that given to it in the book language.

The figures at the end of phrases and sentences denote the Final Particle which is used in the Chinese. The numbers correspond with the numbers of the list of Final Particles towards the end of the book.

ꜞ = The upper even tone, the 上平, as 天, ꜞt'ín

ꜛ = The upper rising tone, the 上上, as 水, ꜛshöü.

ꜗ = The upper retiring, or receding tone, the 上去, as 去, höü ꜗ.

ꜘ = The upper entering tone, the 上入, as 德, tak ꜘ

꜐ = The lower even tone, the 下平, as 人, ꜐yan.

꜑ = The lower rising tone, the 下上, as 我, ꜑ngo.

²= The lower retiring, or receding tone, the 下去, as 父, fú²

ₒ = The middle entering tone, the 中入, as 角, kok ₒ

₂ = The lower entering tone, the 下入, as 月, yüt₂

THE VARIANT TONES.

ₒ = The variant tone of the 上平, or upper even, as 孫, ₒsün. *

ꜛ = The variant tone of the 上上, or upper rising, as 洗, ꜛsaí. *

ꜗ = The variant tone of the 上去, or upper retiring or receding, as 遇, kwo ꜗ *

₂ = The variant tone of the 上入, or upper entering tone, as 識, shik ₂ *

₀₁ = The variant tone of the 中入, or middle entering tone, as 跌, tít ₀₁ *

ₑ = The variant tone of the 下平, or lower entering tone, as ₑyan. *

ₑ = The variant tone of the 下上, or lower rising tone, as 母, ₑmò. *

⁵ = The variant tone of the 下去, or lower retiring or receding tone, as 話, wa⁵ *

₅ = The variant tone of the 下入, or lower entering tone, as 食, shik₅. *

ꜙ = The tone for 廿 and also for 卅, etc., if pronounced as one word, as yá ꜙ .

THE NUMERALS.

		Complicated form.	Simple form.	Running hand.
1.	1	壹	一	
2.	2	貳	二	
3.	3	叄	三	
4.	4	肆	四	
5.	5	伍	五	
6.	6	陸	六	
7.	7	柒	七	
8.	8	捌	八	
9.	9	玖	九	
10.	10	拾	十	
11.	11	拾壹, or 壹拾壹	十一 or 一十一	
12.	12	拾貳, or 壹拾貳	十二 or 一十二	
13.	13	拾叄, or 壹拾叄	十三 or 一十三	
14.	20	貳拾	二十, or 廿	
15.	21	貳拾壹	二十一, or 廿一	
16.	22	貳拾貳	二十二, or 廿二	
17.	30	叄拾	三十, or 卅呀	
18.	31	叄拾壹	三十一, or 卅呀一	
19.	40	肆拾	四十, or 四呀	
20.	79	柒拾玖	七十九, or 七呀九	
21.	84	捌拾肆	八十四, or 八呀四	
22.	96	玖拾陸	九十六, or 九呀六	
23.	100	壹佰	一百	
24.	101	壹佰零壹	一百零一	
25.	110	佰壹, or 壹佰壹拾	百一 or 一百一十	
26.	111	壹佰壹拾壹	一百一十一	
27.	200	貳佰	二百	
28.	300	叄佰	三百	
29.	1,000	壹仟	一千	
30.	10,000	壹萬	一萬	
31.	100,000	拾萬	十萬	
32.	1,000,000	壹佰萬 or 佰萬	一百萬 or 百萬	

1. Note these contracted forms for the tens are not used alone in colloquial, but precede some other word, as, 卅呀錢 ‚Sá-á² (or sá`) ‚ts'in,* thirty cash. When nothing follows thirty, 三十 ‚Sám shap‚ should be used. All these contractions for tens when sounded very rapidly would be considered as one word. If one chooses to consider them as such, the tone might be called a falling tone and represented by one syllable, as above.

2. Or yat‚ shap‚ yat‚, yat‚ shap‚ yí² etc., very often.

THE NUMERALS.

1.	Yat$_{,}$.	One.
2.	Yí^2.	Two.
3.	$_{c}$Sám.	Three.
4.	Sz,.	Four.
5.	^{c}Ng.	Five.
6.	Luk$_2$.	Six.
7.	Ts'at$_{,}$.	Seven.
8.	Pát$_{o}$.	Eight.
9.	^{c}Kaú.	Nine.
10.	Shap$_2$ *or* yat$_{,}$ shap$_2$.	Ten, *or* one ten.
11.	Shap$_2$ yat$_{,}$, *or* yat$_{,}$ shap$_2$ yat$_{,}$.	Ten one, *or* one ten one.
12.	Shap$_2$ yí^2, *or* yat$_{,}$ shap$_2$ yí^2.	Ten two, *or* one ten two.
13.	Shap$_2$ $_{c}$sám, *or* yat$_{,}$ shap$_2$ $_{c}$sám.	Ten three, *or* one ten three.
14.	Yí^2 shap$_2$ *Often abbreviated to* Yá^2.	Two tens, *or* twenty.
15.	Yí^2 shap$_2$ yat$_{,}$ „ Yá^2 yat$_{,}$.	Two tens one, *or* twenty-one.
16.	Yí^2 shap$_2$ yí^2. „ Yá^{2}yí^2.	Two tens two, *or* twenty-two.
17.	$_{c}$Sám shap$_2$. „ $_{c}$Sá-á^2. [1]	Three tens, *or* thirty.
18.	$_{c}$Sám shap$_2$ yat$_{,}$. „ $_{c}$Sá-á^2 yat$_{,}$.	Three tens one, *or* thirty-one.
19.	Sz, shap$_2$. „ Sz,-á^2.	Four tens, *or* forty.
20.	Ts'at$_{,}$ shap$_2$ ^{c}kaú. „ Ts'at$_{,}$-á^2 ^{c}kaú.	Seven tens nine, *or* seventy-nine.
21.	Pát$_{o}$ shap$_2$ sz,. „ Pát$_{o}$-á^2 sz,.	Eight tens four, *or* eighty-four.
22.	^{c}Kaú shap$_2$ luk$_2$. „ ^{c}Kaú-á^2 luk$_2$.	Nine tens six, *or* ninety-six.
23.	Yat$_{,}$ pák$_{o}$.	One hundred.
24.	Yat$_{,}$ pák$_{o}$ $_{c}$leng† yat$_{,}$.	One hundred and one.
25.	Pák$_{o}$ yat, *or* yat$_{,}$ pák$_{o}$ yat$_{,}$.	Hundred one (ten *understood*), *or* one hundred
26.	Yat$_{,}$ pák$_{o}$ yat$_{,}$ shap$_2$ yat$_{,}$.	One hundred one ten one. [one.
27.	Yí^2 pák$_{o}$.	Two hundred.
28.	$_{c}$Sám pák$_{o}$.	Three hundred.
29.	Yat$_{,}$ $_{c}$ts'ín.	One thousand.
30.	Yat$_{,}$ mán^2.	One myriad.
31.	Shap$_2$ mán^2, *or* yat$_{,}$ shap$_2$ mán^2.	Ten myriads, *or* one ten myriads.
32.	Pák$_{o}$ mán^2, *or* yat$_{,}$ pák$_{o}$ mán^2.	One hundred myriads.

---

1. This is pronounced in two ways : when spoken rapidly as if it were only one syllable, as, *sá* ^{c}; but when uttered more slowly it resolves itself into two as given above. See note on opposite page.

LESSON I.—Domestic.

1.	Bring a cup of tea.	揗杯茶嚟、
2.	Serve dinner (or any meal).	起餐喇、
3.	Call the house-coolie.	叫管店嚟、
4.	I want to bathe.	我要洗身咯、
5.	There is no water.	冇水瞒、
6.	Have you had your rice? Thanks, I have.	食飯唔曾呀、唔該咯、食咯、
7.	No; I have not.	唔曾食
8.	Is there any beef? There is no beef.	有牛肉冇呢、冇牛肉咯、
9.	There is mutton	有羊肉呀、
10.	The bread is sour.	麵包酸咯、
11.	Ah! is it?	啊、係咩、
12.	Bring some hot water	揗啲熱水嚟、
13.	I don't want wine	我唔愛酒呀、
14.	The cook hasn't come back yet	做廚未曾翻嚟呀、
15.	Is there any milk?	有牛奶冇叮、
16.	There is a little	有啲咯、
17.	Is it good?	好唔好呀、
18.	It is not the very best, it is not very good, only middling.	唔係十分 (or 至) 好、唔係幾好、中中啲嘒
19.	Put it there.	擸 (or 放在) 咁處咯、
20.	Those are fowls' eggs.	個啲係鷄蛋呀、
21.	They are bad; they are spoilt.	唔好咯;係臭嘅、
22.	How is that? It is very strange.	點解呢、好出奇嘅咯、
23.	Is this good to eat? It is. Thanks	好食嗎、好食叮、唔該呀、
24.	Are there any fowls? There are capons and hens.	有鷄冇呢、有鐭鷄、有鷄嫲咯、
25.	What is this? Give me some.	呢啲係乜野呢、俾啲我喇、
26.	Thank you. Is there any more?	多謝你咯、重有冇呢、
27.	There is. The cook has come.	重有啲 火頭嚟咯、
28.	Who is he? Does he smoke?	佢係乜人、佢食烟咩、
29.	I don't know certainly. Probably he does.	唔知得實咯、怕係有、
30.	The boy has gone out to buy vegetables, and or meat.	事仔出街買餸呀、
31.	Has he bought pork or vegetables?	佢係買猪肉、嘅菜呢、
32.	He is a Chinese, and comes from Fat-shan.	佢係唐人、喺佛山嚟嘅、

LESSON I.—Domestic.

1. ͻNing ͻpōŭ ͼch'á ͼlaí.	Bring cup tea come.
2. ꞌHéí ts'án ͻlá.²	Get-up meal.²
3. Kíú꞊ ꞌkwún-tím꞊ (or tím³•) ͼlaí.	Call house-coolie (or shop-coolie) come.
4. ꞔNgo yíú꞊ ꞌsaí ͻshan lok ᵒ.	I want wash body.³²
5. ꞔMò ꞌshōŭ po꞊. [shik₅• lok ᵒ.	No water.⁶⁰
6. Shik₅• fán² ͼm ͼts'ang á꞊? ͼM-ͼkoí lok ᵒ.	Ate rice not yet eh?² Beg-pardon,³², eaten.³²
7. ͼM ͼts'ang shik₂. [The tone does not change here.] [yuk₂ lok ᵒ.	Not yet eat. [No beef.³²
8. ꞔYaú ͼngaú-yuk₂ ꞔmò ͼni ?² ꞔMò ͼngaú-	Have beef (lit. ox, or cow meat) not eh?⁵³
9. ꞔYaú ͼyōng-yuk₂ á꞊.	Have mutton (lit. sheep meat).²
10. Mín²-ᵒpáú ͼsün lok ᵒ.	Bread sour.³²
11. ͼO! Haí² ͼme ?²	Ah! 'tis is-it?³⁹
12. ͼNing ͼti¹ yít₂ ꞌshōŭ ͼlaí.	Bring some hot water come.
13. ꞔNgo ͼm oí꞊ ͼtsaú á꞊.	I not want wine.²
14. Tsò²-ͼch'ü• méí² ͼts'ang ͼfán ͼlaí á꞊.	Cook not yet back come.²
15. ꞔYaú ͼngaú ꞔnáí ꞔmò ͼá ?²	Have cow's milk not eh?¹
16. ꞔYaú ͼti lok ᵒ.	Have little.³²
17. ꞌHò ͼm ͼhò á꞊?	Good not good eh?²
18. ͼM haí² shap₂ ͼfan (or chí꞊) ꞌhò; ͼm haí² ꞌkéí ꞌhò; chung- chung-téí³• chek ᵒ.	Not is ten parts (or very) good (or best); not is very good; middling only.⁷
19. ͼChaí (or fong꞊ tsoí²) ꞌko shü꞉ lok ᵒ.	Place (or place on) that place.³²
20. Ko꞉²- ti haí² ͼkaí-tán³• á꞊.	Those are fowls' eggs.²
21. ͼM ꞌhò lok ᵒ; haí² ch'aú꞊ ke꞉.	Not good ;³² are stinking.¹⁵
22. ꞌTím ꞌkáí ͼni?² ꞌHò ch'ut₂-ͼk'éí ke꞉ lok ᵒ.	How explain eh?⁵³ Very extraordinary.¹⁵ ³²
23. ꞌHò shik₂ ꞔmá? ꞌHò shik₂ ͼá.² ͼM ͼkoí á꞊.	Good eat isn't-it ?²² Good eat.² Not proper.²
24. ꞔYaú ͼkaí (or ͼkaí) ꞔmò ͼni?² ꞔYaú sín꞊- ͼkaí (or ͼkaí), ꞔyaú ͼkaí [No change in tone here]-ͼná •lok ᵒ. [ͼlá.²	Have fowls not eh?⁵³ Have capons, have hens.³²
25. ͼNi- ti haí² ͼmi³-ꞔye ͼni?² ꞌPéí ͼti ꞔngo	This is what-thing eh?⁵³ Give some me.²¹
26. ͼTo tse² ꞔnéí lok ᵒ. Chung² ꞔyaú ꞔmò ͼni ?²	Many thanks to-you.² More have no eh?⁵³
27. Chung² ꞔyaú ͼti. ꞌFo-ͼt'aú• ͼlaí lok ᵒ.	Besides have some. Cook come.³²
28. ꞔK'ōŭ haí² ͼmi ͼyan ?• ꞔK'ōŭ shik₂ ᵒyín ͼme ?²	He is what man ? He smokes eh?³⁹
29. ͼM ͼchí-tak₃ shat₂ lok ᵒ. P'á꞊ haí² ꞔyaú.	Not know certainly.³² Fear (it) is (that he) does.
30. Sz²-ꞔtsaí ch'ut₂ ͼkáí (or ͼkáí) ꞔmáí sung꞊ á꞊.	Boy gone-out street buy viands.²
31. ꞔK'ōŭ haí² ꞔmáí ͼchü-yuk₂, péí² ts'oí꞊ ͼni ?²	He has bought pork, or vegetables eh?⁵³
32. ꞔK'ōŭ haí² ͼT'ong ͼyan. ꞌhaí Fat₂-ͼshán ͼlaí ke꞉.	He is T'ong man (i.e. Chinese); from Fat-shan come.¹⁵

1. This word is uniformly spelled *i* in this book, but it must be remembered that it is often pronounced *i* as well.

2. These finals are in either the 上平 or variant of that tone, the highest tone of all, according to the sense or meaning to be conveyed, or emphasis shown.

3. This is a very common contraction of 乜 mat₂, in colloquial.

LESSON II.—General.

1	Come here Why don't you come?	嚟呢處呀、做乜你唔嚟呢、
2	Who has come? Who is it?	乜人嚟吖、乜誰吖、 *or* 邊個吖、
3	No one has come.	冇人嚟吖 *or* 冇人呀 *or* 冇邊個吖、
4	Who is that?	嗰個係乜人呢、
5	I don't know. How should I know? [man.	唔知呀、我點知呀、
6	He is not a good man. He is a very bad	佢係唔好人呀、佢係好惡人嚟、
7	Tell him to go away.	叫佢扯咯、
8	He has gone. He went long ago	佢去咗咯、去好耐咯、
9	Close the door, don't fasten it.	掩埋門、咪閂吖、
10	Open the door. Why did you lock it?	開門呀、做乜你鎖呢、
11	Tell the Amah to come to me.	叫亞媽嚟見我喇、
12	Come quickly; the quicker the better.	快啲嚟、越快越好咯、
13	Where's the coolie; has he come?	咎店呢、嚟未曾呀、
14	Come to-morrow, or the day after to-morrow.	聽日嚟喇、後日嚟都好吖(*or* 都做得吖)、
15	There is only a very little.	有少少咯、
16	It's good is it? He says so.	好嘛嗎、佢係噉話、
17	What does he say? Tell me.	佢話乜野、講過我聽喇、
18	He says he doesn't wish to come. [with me.	佢話唔想嚟咯、
19	Explain to him that he must certainly go	解明過佢聽、是必要同我去、
20	How many persons are there, old and	唔論大細、有幾多人呢、
21	More than ten. [young?	有十幾個、 *or* 有十零個咯、*or* 十個有多、
22	Altogether there are sixty men.	喊味吟有六十人咯、
23	Are there any children?	有細仔仔冇呢、
24	There is a boy.	有個(*or* 壹個)仔咯、
25	Is that a boy, or a girl?	嗰個係仔嘅女呢、
26	He is in my employ.	佢喺我處打工嘅、
27	Who is your master?	邊個係你事頭呢、
28	He is a native of the place, that is a Cantonese.	佢係本地人、即係城人咯
29	He is not a fellow-villager of yours.	佢唔係同你同鄉嘅、
30	Where does he live?	佢喺邊處住呢、
31	A long way from here.	離呢處有好遠咯、
32	Do you go by land, or by water?	打路去嘅搭船去呢、

1. Or as in No. 2.

2. 聽日 ₍t'ing yat₂ very often also means any indefinite time in the future.

LESSON II.—General.

1. ₍Lai ₍ni shū⁾ á⁾. Tsò²-mat₎ ⁵néi ₍m ₍lai ₍ni?² [ko⁾ ₀á?²	Come this place.² Why you not come eh?53 [eh?¹
2. Mi ₍yan• ₍lai ₍á?² Mi-₍shōŭ• ₍á?² ₀Pín	What man come eh?¹ Who eh?¹ Which one
3. ⁵Mò ₍yan ₍lai ₍á,² or simply ⁵Mò ₍yan ₍á,² or ⁵Mò pín ko⁾ ₀á.²	No man come,¹ or no man,¹ or no which [C.] ¹
4. ⁵Ko ko⁾ haí² ₍mi ₍yan• ₍ni?²	That [C.] is what man eh?53
5. ₍M ₍chí á⁾. ⁵Ngo ⁵tím ₍chí á⁾?	Not know.² I how know eh?² [man.14
6. ⁵K·öŭ haí² ₍m ⁵hò ₍yan á⁾. ⁵K·öŭ haí²	He is not good man.² He is very wicked.
7. Kíú⁾ ⁵k·öŭ ⁵ch'e lok₀. [⁵hò ok₀ ₍yan ká⁾.	Tell him to-be-off.32
8. ⁵K·öŭ höŭ⁾-⁵cho lok₀. Höŭ⁾ •⁵hò noí²	He gone [s. of p. t.].32 Gone very long.32
9. ⁵Yím ₍maí ₍mún, ⁵maí ₍shán ₍á.² [lok₀.	Close to door, don't fasten it.¹
10. ₍Hoí ₍mún á⁾. Tsò²-mat₎ ⁵néi ⁵so ₍ni?²	Open door.² Why you lock eh?53
11. Kíú⁾ Á⁾-⁵Má ₍laí kín⁾ ⁵ngo ₍lá.²	Call Amah [this also means grandmother if in lower even tone, as Á⁾ ₍má] come see me.21
12. Fáí⁾-₍ti ₍laí: yūt₎ fáí⁾ yūt₎ ⁵hò lok₀.	Quickly come: still quicker still better.32
13. ⁵Kwún tím⁾• ₍ni²; ₍laí meí² ₍ts'ang á⁾?	House (or shop) coolie eh;53 come not yet eh?²
14. ₍T'ing [better ₍T'ing]-yat₎ ₍laí ₍lá,² haú²-yat₎ ₍laí ₀tò ⁵hò ₍á,² (or ₀tò tsò² tak₎	To-morrow come.21 Day-after-to-morrow come also good,¹ (or also do can¹).
15. ⁵Yaú ⁵shíú ⁵shíú che.² [₍á²).	Have little little only.7
16. ⁵Hò lá⁾ ⁵má? ⁵K·öŭ haí² ⁵kòm wá².	Good ?23 37 He does so say.
17. ⁵K·öŭ wá² ₍mi ⁵ye? ⁵Kong kwo⁾ ⁵ngo ₍t'engt ₍lá.²	He says what thing? Tell over to-me to-hear.21
18. ⁵K·öŭ wá² ₍m ⁵söng ₍laí lok₀.	He says not wish come.32
19. ⁵Káí ₍ming kwo⁾ ⁵k·öŭ ₍t'engt shí²-pít₎ yíú⁾ ₍t'ung ⁵ngo höŭ⁾.	Explain clearly to him to-hear certainly must with me go. [men eh?53
20. ₍M lun² táí² saí⁾ ⁵yaú ⁵kéí ₍to ₍yan• ₍ni?²	No matter (whether) big small have how many
21. ⁵Yaú shap₎ ⁵kéí ko⁾, or ⁵yaú shap₎ ₍lengt ko⁾ lok₀, or shap₎ ko⁾ ⁵yaú ₀to.	Have ten odd [C.], or have ten plus [C.],34 or ten [C.] have more.
22. Hám²-páng²₁-láng² ⁵yaú luk₎-shap₎ ₍yan lok₀. [⁵mò ₍ni?²	In-all have sixty men.32
23. ⁵Yaú saí⁾ (or more often ⁵sam)- ₍man-⁵tsaí.	Have children not eh?53
24. ⁵Yaú ko⁾ (or yat₎ ko⁾) ⁵tsaí lok₀.	Have [C.] (or one [C.]) boy.32
25. ⁵Ko ko⁾ haí² ⁵tsaí, péí² ⁷nöŭ• ₍ni?²	That [C.] is boy, or girl eh?53
26. ⁵K·öŭ ⁵haí ⁵ngo shū⁾ ⁵tá-₍kung ke⁾.	He at my place works.15
27. ₀Pín ko⁾ haí² ⁵néí sz²-₎t'aú• ₍ni?²	Which [C.] is your master eh?53
28. ⁵K·öŭ haí² ⁵pún téí² ₍yan, tsik₎ haí² ₍sheng•t ₍yan lok₀. [ke.⁾	He is native soil man, that is city man.32
29. ⁵K·öŭ ₍m haí² ₍t'ung ⁵néí ₍t'ung ₍höng-	He not is with you together villager.15
30. ⁵K·öŭ ⁵haí pín shū⁾ chū² ₍ni?²	He at what place lives eh?53
31. ₍Léí ₍ni shū⁾ ⁵yaú ⁵hò ⁵yün lok₀.	Separated-from this place have very far.32
32. ⁵Tá lò² höŭ⁾, péí² táp₀ ₍shün höŭ⁾ ₍ni?²	By road go, or on ship go eh?53

1. This word is pronounced pá² when spoken rapidly.

2. These finals may be either in the 上平 or in the variant tone, higher than the 上平; for example, the sentence may bè Tsò² mat₎ ⁵néí ₍m ₍laí ₍ni? or Tsò² mat₎ ⁵néí ₍m ₍laí ₍ni? according to the sense or emphasis to be conveyed.

LESSON III.—General.

1.	What o'clock is it?	幾點鐘呢、
2	O! it's half-past ten.	呀、十點半咯、
3.	Come back at four o'clock	四點翻嚟喇、
4.	Tell him to wait.　Wait.	叫佢等吓、等一吓喇、
5.	Come by-and-bye.	等吓嚟、
6.	He says you must wait.	佢話你要等呀、
7.	When are you going out?	你幾時出街呢、
8.	It's very hot to-day.	今日好熱呀、
9.	It's not very hot.	唔係十分熱嘅、
10.	It was rather hot yesterday as well	昨日都係幾熱呀、
11.	To-day is hotter than yesterday.	今日熱過昨日咯、
12.	Next month will be cold.	第二個月(係)冷嚟、
13.	To-morrow is the end of the month.	聽日月尾嘞、
14.	It was very cold last night.	昨晚真正冷嚟、
15.	Is this a long, or short month?	呢個月大嘅月小呢、
16.	There was a typhoon some days ago	先幾日打風颶、
17.	Is there any wind now?	而家有風冇呢、
18.	It's raining now. It's only a slight shower.	呢陣落雨嚟、落雨微呎、
19.	Bring me an umbrella.　There is no need.	掉把遮俾我、唔使呀、
20.	It rains heavily in summer (or hot weather).	天熱落大雨咯、
21.	I want to go out in the afternoon.　[chair.	我下晝要出街、
22.	Call the coolies to come and carry the	叫抬轎佬 (or 轎夫) 嚟抬轎、
23.	Are there any horses here?	呢處有馬冇呢、
24.	I think they are not particularly good.　I fancy they are pretty good.	我估唔多好嘅、都幾好嘅、
25.	The sun is intensely hot to-day　There are no clouds hiding it.	熱頭今日好猛、冇雲遮住咯、
26.	It's too hot　I dare not go out in the day-	熱過頭、我日頭唔敢行街、
27.	Call some one to pull the punkah.　[time.	叫人嚟(扯 or 搇)風扇呀、
28.	You needn't pull it. You have no strength.	你唔使扯吖、你冇力吖、
29.	It's only a trifling matter.　It's no matter.	閒事嚟、冇相干咯、
30.	I'm afraid I shall catch cold.　I feel very cold.	我慌冷親呀、我見好冷呀、
31.	I am in a perspiration.　It's very hard work to take a walk when it is so hot.	出汗咯、咁熱行街見好辛苦咯、
32.	The climate does not suit me.	呢處水士唔合我咯、

LESSON III.—General.

1.	ᶜKéi ᶜtím ꜀chung ꜀ni ? 2	What stroke clock, eh ?53
2.	꜀O, shap$_2$ ᶜtím pún˒ lok꜀. 1	Ah ! Ten stroke half. 32
3.	Sz˒ ᶜtím ꜀fán ꜀lái ꜀lá. 2 [ᶜhá*) ꜀lá. 2	Four o'clock back come.21
4.	Kíú˒ ᶜk'öü ᶜtang ᶜhá. ᶜTang yat˒ ᶜhá (*or*	Tell him wait little. Wait a little.21
5.	ᶜTang ꜀há (*or* ꜀há) ꜀laí.	Wait a-bit come.
6.	ᶜK'öü wá^2 ᶜnéí yíú˒ ᶜtang á˒.	He says you must wait.2
7.	ᶜNéí ᶜkéi-꜀shí* ch'ut˒ ꜀káí (*or* ꜀káí) ꜀ni ? 2	You what-time go-out street eh ?53
8.	꜀Kam-yat$_2$ ᶜhò yít$_2$ o˒.	To-day very hot.56
9.	꜀M haí^2 shap$_2$ ꜀fan yít$_2$ ká˒.	Not is ten parts hot.14
10.	Tsok$_2$-yat$_2$ ꜀tò haí^2 ᶜkéi yít$_2$ ꜀á. 2	Yesterday also was somewhat hot.1
11.	꜀Kam-yat$_2$ (*often pronounced* mat$_2$) yít$_2$ kwo˒ tsok$_2$-yat$_2$ (*or* ꜀ts'am-mat$_2$) lok꜀.	To-day hotter than yesterday. 32
12.	Taí^2-yí^2-ko˒ yüt$_2$ (haí^2)[3] ᶜláng lo˒.	Next (*or* another) [*C.*] month (will be) cold.31
13.	꜀T'ing (*or* ꜀T'ing)-yat$_2$ yüt$_2$ ᶜméí lá˒.	To-morrow month end.22
14.	Tsok$_2$ (*often pronounced* ꜀ts'am) ᶜmán ꜀chan ching˒ ᶜláng lo˒.	Last night truly really cold.31
15.	꜀Ni-ko˒ yüt$_2$ taí^2, péí^2 yüt$_2$ ᶜsíú ꜀ni ? 2	This month large, or month small, eh ?53
16.	꜀Sín (*or* ꜀Sín) ᶜkéi yat$_2$ ᶜtá ꜀fung-kaú^2.	Before (*or* a number of days ago) several days,
17.	꜀Yí-꜀ká ᶜyaú ꜀fung ᶜmò ꜀ni ?2 [꜀che 2.	Now have wind not, eh ?53 [strike typhoon.
18.	꜀Ni chan˒* lok$_2$ ᶜyü lo˒. Lok$_2$ ᶜyü ꜀méí	This-time fall rain.31 Fall rain fine only.7
19.	꜀Ning ᶜpá ꜀che ᶜpéí ᶜngo. ꜀M ᶜshaí á˒.	Bring (*C.*) umbrella give me. Not need.2
20.	꜀T'ín yít$_2$ lok$_2$ taí^2 ᶜyü lok꜀. ꜀káí).	Weather hot falls great rain.32
21.	ᶜNgo há^2-chaú˒ yíú˒ ch'ut˒ ꜀káí (*or* better	I afternoon want-to go-out street. [carry chair.
22.	Kíú˒ ꜀t'oí kíú˒* ᶜlò (*or* kíú˒* ꜀fú) ꜀laí ꜀t'oí	Call carry chair fellows (*or* chair bearers) come
23.	꜀Ni shü˒ ᶜyaú ᶜmá ᶜmò ꜀ni ? 2 kíú˒*.	This place have horse not, eh ?53
24.	ᶜNgo ᶜkwú ꜀m ꜀to ᶜhò kwá˒. ꜀Tò ᶜkéi ᶜhò kwá˒. [꜀wan ꜀che-chü^2 lok꜀.	I think not very good probably.18 Also pretty good I-think.18
25.	Yít$_2$-꜀t'aú* ꜀kam-yat$_2$ ᶜhò ᶜmáng. ᶜMò	Sun to-day very fierce. No clouds hide.32
26.	Yít$_2$ kwo˒*-꜀t'aú ᶜngo yat$_2$-꜀t'aú* ꜀m ᶜkòm ꜀háng† ꜀káí (*or* ꜀káí). [shín˒ á˒.	Hot over-much I daytime not dare walk streets.
27.	Kíú˒ ꜀yan ꜀laí (*or* ꜀mang) ᶜch'e, ꜀fung-	Call man come pull punkah.2
28.	ᶜNéí ꜀m ᶜshaí ᶜch'e ꜀á. 2. ᶜNéí ᶜmò lik$_2$ ꜀á. 2	You not need pull.1 You no strength.1
29.	꜀Hán sz^2 ꜀che 2 ; ᶜmò ꜀sõng-꜀kòn lok꜀.	Trifling matter only 7 ; no importance.32
30.	ᶜNgo ꜀fong ᶜláng ꜀ts'an á˒. ᶜNgo kín˒ ᶜhò ᶜláng á˒.	I fear cold catch.2 I feel very cold.2
31.	Ch'ut˒-hòn^2 lok꜀. Kòm˒ yít$_2$ ꜀háng† ꜀káí (*or* better ꜀káí) kín˒ ᶜhò ꜀san-ᶜfú lok꜀.	Perspire.32 So hot walk streets feel very distressing.32
32.	꜀Ni shü˒ ᶜshöü ᶜt'ò ꜀m hòp$_2$ ᶜngo lo˒.	This place water soil not agree me. 32

1. Let the learner remember that this final *k* is scarcely heard.
2. See note to Lessons I and II.
3. The verb may, or may not be used, and so in similar sentences throughout the book.

LESSON IV.—General.

1.	What is this?	呢啲係也野呢、
2.	This is butter.	呢啲係牛油嚧、
3	Is there any fruit?	有菓子右呀、
4.	There are only two kinds.	有兩樣嘅、
5.	Are there not several kinds?	唔係有幾樣咩、
6.	No: there are plantains and pine-apples	右、有蕉有波羅、
7.	Are there no other kinds?	右第二樣咩、
8.	There are no other kinds.	右第二樣略、
9.	Bring a light. I'll trouble you for a light *(for my cigar or pipe)*.	**掉火嚟、唔該你借個火我、**
10.	Where did this letter come from?	呢封信喺邊處嚟呢、
11.	From the Tak-kee hong	喺德記行嚟嘅、
12.	Is there any answer?	有囘音右呀、
13.	There is no answer.	右囘音羅、
14.	Bring me a chair.	掉張椅俾我、
15.	Put it on the table.	擠在檯面、
16.	Nonsense! Why are you so silly?	咻、做也你咁衰叮、嘍、整成個 **[啲衰樣**[1]
17.	I am only jesting Do you think it	我講笑話咋、你見怪咩、
18.	Bring me a pen and ink. [strange?	掉筆墨嚟俾我喇、
19.	I think there is a pencil up stairs.	樓上 (*or* 樓) 有支筆哦、
20.	Is there anyone down stairs? Go down	樓下有人右呢、落去睇吓、
21.	This house has seven rooms. [and see.	呢間屋有七間房呀、
22.	Has it a garden? Where is the gardener?	有花園右呢、花王喺邊處、
23.	It has a small garden	有個細花園呀、
24.	Where is your master? He is out.	事頭呢、出街羅、
25.	How long has he been gone?	佢出街有幾耐呢、
26.	When will he be back?	幾時翻嚟呢、
27.	He didn't say.	佢又右話幾時翻嚟嘍 (*or* 右話、)
28.	Is your mistress at home? [master.[1]	女事頭 (*or* 女東家[2]) 喺處唔喺處呢、
29.	She is not here; she went out with my	唔喺處、佢同東家出街略、
30.	Go with me to find him. I can't go.	孖我去揾佢喇、我唔去得叮、
31.	I can't. I'm busy. I have no time	唔得呀、有事叮、唔得閒叮、
32.	Come again to-night. Don't come so late.	今晚又嚟喇、咪咁夜嚟呀、

1. The first of these sentences is what a woman would say; the second, what a man would say.

2. The second is a more polite form, though the first is most commonly used

LESSON IV.—General.

1.	꜀Ni-ₒti haí² ꜀mi ꜀ye ꜀ni ? ²	This is what thing, eh ? ⁵³
2.	꜀Ni-ₒti haí² ꜀ngaú-꜀yaú po³.	This is butter (lit. cow's oil). ⁶⁰
3.	꜀Yaú ꜀kwo-꜀tsz ꜀mò á³ ?	Have fruit not, eh? ²
4.	꜀Yaú ꜀löng yõng² ꜂che. ²	Have two kinds only. ⁷
5.	꜄M haí² ꜀yaú ꜀kéi yõng² ꜄me ? ²	Not is have several kinds, is-it-not ? ³⁹ or Is it not that there are several kinds ?
6.	꜀Mò, ꜀yaú tsíú. ꜀yaú po-꜀lo¹.	No, have plantains, have pineapples.
7.	꜀Mò taí²-yí² yõng² ꜀me ? ²	No second kind, eh ? ³⁹
8.	꜀Mò taí²-yí² yõng² lok ₒ. [꜀ngo.	No second kind. ³²
9.	꜀Ning ꜀fo ꜀lai. ꜀M-꜀koi ꜀néi tse³ ko³ ꜀fo	Bring fire come. Trouble you lend a light to-
10.	Ni ꜀fung-sun³ ꜀hai ꜀p:n shü³ ꜀lai ꜀ni ? ²	This [C.] letter from what place come, eh ? ⁵³
11.	꜀Hai Tak-꜀kéí ꜄hong⁰ ꜀lai ke³.	From Tak-kéi hong come. ¹⁵
12.	꜀Yaú ꜀wúi-꜀yam ꜀mò á³ ?	Have answer not, eh ? ²
13.	꜀Mò ꜀wúí-꜀yam lo³	No answer. ³¹
14.	꜀Ning ꜀chöng ꜀yi ꜀péi ꜀ngo	Bring [C.] chair give me.
15.	꜀Chaí tso:² ꜀t'oi min³⁰ (or ꜀t'oi without mín³⁰).	Place on table face.
16.	Ts'oi! Tsò²-mat, ꜀néi kòm³ ꜀shöü á³ ? ³ Ts'ai ! ꜀ching ꜀sheng+ ko³-꜀ti shöü yõng³. ⁰³	Nonsense ! Why you so silly, eh ? ¹ Nonsense ! Make complete that silly style !
17.	꜀Ngo ꜀konʒ síú wá³⁰ ꜂che³. ꜀Néi kin³ kwáí³ ꜀me ? 2	I speak laughing words only. ⁸ You perceive strange, eh ? ³⁹
18.	꜀Ning pat, mak, ꜀lai ꜀péi ꜀ngo ꜀lá. ²	Bring pencil, ink come give me. ²¹
19.	꜀Laú-shöng² (or ꜀laú⁰) ꜀yaú chi pat, kwá³.	Upstairs have [C.] pencil I-think. ¹⁸
20.	꜀Laú-há² ꜀yaú ꜀yan ꜀mò ꜀ni ? Lok, höü³ ꜀t'aí ꜀há.	Downstairs have man not, eh ? Down go see a-bit.
21.	Ni ꜀kán uk, ꜀yaú ts'at, kán ꜀fong⁰ á³.	This [C.] house has seven [C.] rooms. ²
22.	꜀Yaú fá-꜀yün⁰ ꜀mò ꜀ni ? ² Fá (or ꜀fá) ꜀wong ꜀hai ꜀pín shü³ ?	Have flower-garden not, eh ? ⁵³ Flower king at what place ?
23.	꜀Yaú ko³ saí³ ꜀fá-꜀yün⁰ á³.	Have a small flower-garden. ²
24.	Sz²-꜀t'aú⁰ ꜀ni ? Ch'ut, ꜀kái lo³. [꜀ni ? ²	Master, eh ? ⁵³ Gone-out street. ³¹
25.	꜀K'öü ch'ut, ꜀kái (or ₒkáí) ꜀yaú ꜀kéí noí³⁰ ꜀	He go-out street have how long, eh ? ⁵³
26.	꜀Kéí ꜀shí⁰ fán ꜀lai ꜀ni ? ²	What time back come, eh ? ⁵³
27.	꜀K'öü yaú² ꜀mò wá² ꜀kéí ꜄shí⁰ ꜀fán ꜀lai po³ (or ꜀mò wá²).	He even not say what time back come ⁶⁰ (or not say).
28.	꜀Nöü-sz²-꜀t'aú (or better ꜀nöü-꜀tung-꜀ka) ꜀haí shü³, ꜀m ꜀haí shü³, ꜀ni ? ²	Mistress at place, not at place, eh ? ⁵³
29.	꜀M ꜀haí shü³; ꜀k'öü ꜀t'ung ꜀tung ꜀ká ch'ut, ꜀káí (or ꜀káí) lok ₒ.	Not at place ; she with master go-out street. ⁵³
30.	Má³ ꜀ngo höü³ ꜀wan ꜀k'öü ꜀lá. ² ꜀Ngo ꜀m höü³ tak, á.	With me go find (or look for) him. ²¹ I not go can. ¹
31.	꜀M tak, á³. ꜀Yaú sz² ꜀á. ꜀M tak,꜄hán ꜀á. ²	Not can. ² Have business. ¹ Not have leisure. ¹
32.	꜀Kam-꜀mán⁰ yaú² ꜀lai ꜀lá. ² ꜀Maí kòm³ ye² ꜀laí á³.	To-night again come. ²¹ Don't so late come. ²

1. It is better to keep to the original tone here.   2.   See note on previous pages.
3. The first sentence is what a woman would say ; the second what a man would say.

LESSON V.—General.

1	What does he say? [hard up for money.	佢話乜野呢、
2.	He says he has no money. He says he is	冇銀喇、銀両緊啊、
3.	Did he say that? Give him some.	佢係咁話咩、俾啲佢喇、
4.	Can you read?	你識字唔識吖、
5.	I can't read. Neither can I write.	唔識咯、我又唔曉寫字添、
6.	Ask the teacher to come.	請先生嚟喇、
7.	What is your surname? *(To an inferior)* What is your surname?	高姓呀、你姓乜呢、
8.	My surname is Wong.	小姓黃、*or* 姓黃、
9.	Can you speak Chinese?	你噲講唐話唔嗜呢、
10.	I can. What's your name?	噲吖、你叫(做)乜名呢、
11.	My name is A-Luk.	我名叫(做)亞六、*or* 我叫做亞六、
12.	He is an Englishman.	佢係英國人呀、
13.	You are a native of the place.	你係本地人咯、 [旗人、
14.	He is an American.	佢係美國人、*or* (more commonly) 花
15.	How many Chinese are there?	有幾多唐人呀、
16.	Do you like this?	你中意呢啲唔中意呀、
17.	Do you like being here?	你中意喺呢處唔中意呢、
18.	I do. It would be well to be here always.	中意吖、時時喺處都好呀、
19.	Tell him to go back. He cannot come.	叫佢翻去嘞、佢唔做得嚟、
20.	Seize that man. If you don't, he will run off.	拉嗰個人喇、唔係佢就走咯、
21.	What has he been doing? *or* What does [he do?	佢做乜野吖、
22.	He is a thief.	佢做賊咯 (*or* 佢係賊咯、)、
23.	What has he stolen? Is it of value?	佢偷乜野呢、係值錢唔值呢、
24.	He has not stolen anything yet.	唔曾偷倒 (到¹) 野呀、
25.	Has he struck anybody? What did he strike with?	有打人冇呢、係使乜野嚟打呢、
26.	With his hand; he is a very dangerous man.	使手咯、佢好勢兇嘅、
27.	He wanted to snatch that pair of bracelets.	佢想搶個對鈪咯、
28.	Take him to prison. [rattan.	拉佢去坐監喇、
29.	Afterwards give him twenty blows with a	後來打佢二十籐、
30.	Only let him go when he has been beaten.	打咀至好放佢出去咯、
31.	He ought to be sentenced to two weeks' imprisonment.	應該辦佢坐兩個禮拜監吖、
32.	Warn him not to do it again. If he does, he will be more severely punished.	警戒佢咪製過 (*or* 咪再製)、若係再製、就加重嚴辦咯、

---

1. This is the correct character, but the first represents the correct tone.

LESSON V.—General.

1.	ᶜK'öü wá² ₍mi ᶜye ₍ni?²	He says what thing, eh ?⁵³
2.	ᶜMò ₋ngan• wo². ₍Ngan-ᶜlöng ᶜkan wo².	No money he-says.⁶⁵ Money pressing he-says.⁶⁵
3.	ᶜK'öü hai² ᶜkòm wá² ₍me?² Péí ₋ti ᶜk'öü ₍lá.²	He did so say, eh ?³⁹ Give some him.²¹
4.	ᶜNéí shik₍ tsz² ₍m shik₍ á?² [₍t'ím.	You know characters not know, eh ?¹
5.	₍M shik₍ lo². ᶜNgo yaú² ₍m ᶜhíú ᶜse tsz²	Not know.³¹ I besides not understand to-write
6.	ᵀTs'engᵗ Sín-₍shángᵗ ₍laí lá.²	Invite Teacher come.²¹ [character moreover.
7.	₍Kò sing² á²? ᶜNéí sing² mat₍ ni?	Exalted surname, eh ?²Your surname what, eh?⁵³
8.	ᶜSíú sing² ₍Wong, or Sing² ₍Wong.	Diminutive surname Wong, or Surname Wong.
9.	ᶜNéí ᶜwúí ᶜkong₍T'ong wá,⁵• ₍m ᶜwúí ₍ni?²	You can speak Chinese words, not can, eh?⁵⁵
10.	ᶜWúí ₍á;² ᶜnéí kíú² (tsò²) mat ₋meng•ᵗ ₍ni?² [kíú² tsò² Á²-Luk₂.	Can ;¹ you called (to-be) what name, eh ?⁵³
11.	ᶜNgo ₋meng•ᵗ kíú² (tsò²)Á²-Luk₂, or ᶜNgo	My name is-called A-Luk, or I am-called A-Luk.
12.	ᶜK'öü haí² ₍Ying kwok₀ ₍yan á².	He is English nation man.²
13.	ᶜNéí haí² ᶜpún téí² ₍yan lok₀.	You are native soil man.³²
14.	ᶜK'öü haí² ᶜMéí Kwok₀ ₍yan, or ₍Fá ₋k'éí• (or ordinary tone) ₍yan.	He is American country man, or Flowery Flag man.
15.	ᶜYaú ᶜkéí ₀to ₍T'ong-₍yan á²?	Have how many Chinese, eh ?²
16.	ᶜNéí ₍chung-yí² ni-₀ti ₍m chung-yí² á²?	You like this, not-like, eh ?²
17.	ᶜNéí ₍chung-yí² ᶜhaí ₍ni shü² ₍m ₍chung-yí² ₍ni?²	You like being-at this place, not like, eh?⁵³
18.	₍Chung-yí² ₍á.² ᶜShí-₍shí ᶜhaí shü² ₍tò ᶜhò á². [tak₀ ₍laí.	Like.¹ Always in (this) place also good.²
19.	Kíú²ᶜk'öü ₍fán höü² lá². ᶜK'öü ₍m tsò².	Call him back go ²² He not do can come.
20.	₍Laí ᶜko-ko₀ ₍yan (or ₋yan•) ₍lá.² ₍M haí², ᶜk'öü tsaú² ᶜtsaú lok₀.	Arrest that man.²¹ If not, he will-just run.³²
21.	ᶜK'öü tsò² mi-ᶜye á?² [lok₀.]	He does what thing, eh ?¹
22.	ᶜK'öü tsò² ts'ák₂ lok₀; or ᶜK'öü haí² ts'ák₂	He is thief.³²
23.	ᶜK'öü t'aú ₍mi ᶜye ₍ni?² Haí² chik₂ ₋ts'ín• ke, ₍m chik₂ ₍ni?²	He steal what thing, eh ?⁵³ Is worth money, ¹⁵ not worth, eh?⁵³
24.	₍M-₍t'sang t'aú-₍tò ᶜye á².	Not-yet stolen anything.²
25.	ᵀYaú ᶜtá ₍yan, ᶜmò ₍ni?² Haí² ᶜshaí mat₍ ᶜye ₍laí ᶜtá ₍ni? [ke².	Have strike man, not, eh?⁵³ Have use what thing in-order-to strike, eh ?⁵³
26.	ᶜShaí ᶜshaú lok₀. ᶜK'öü ᶜhò shaí²-₍hung	Use hands.³² He very violent.¹⁵
27.	ᶜK'öü ᶜsöng ᶜts'öng ko² töü² ák•₍ lok₀.	He wished snatch that pair bracelets.³²
28.	₍Laí ᶜk'öü höü² ᶜt'sòt₍ kám₍ lá.	Pull him away sit prison.²¹
29.	Haú²-₋loí ᶜtá ᶜk'öü yí²-shap₂ ₋t'ang•	Afterwards beat him twenty rattans.
30.	ᶜTá ᶜcho [s. of p. t.] chí² ᶜhò fong² ᶜk'öü ch'ut₍ höü² lok₀. [páí² ₍kám á².	Beat finished only good loose him out go.³²
31.	₍Ying-₍koí pán² ᶜk'öü ᶜts'òt ᶜlöng ko² ᶜlaí	Ought sentenced him sit two [C.] weeks prison.²
32.	₍King-káí² ᶜk'öü ᶜmaí chaí² kwo², (or ᶜmaí tsoí² chaí²). Yök₂ haí² tsoí² chaí², tsaú² ₍ká ᶜch'ungᵗ ₍yím pán² lok₀.	Warn him not do again (or not again do). If does again do, then add heavily severely punish.³²

LESSON VI.—Relationships.

1.	Who are you?	你係乜人呢。
2.	He is my father.	佢係我老喱咯。
3.	Have you a mother?	你有老母冇呢。
4.	When did you marry?	你幾時娶親呢。
5.	More than ten years ago.	十幾年, or 十年有多囉。
6.	Have you any children?	有仔女冇呀。
7.	I have several daughters, but no sons	有幾個女, 冇仔。
8.	How old is the eldest?	至大(or 至大個, or 嘅)有幾大呢。
9.	She is between ten and twenty.	今年有十幾歲。
10.	Is she married?	嫁咗(or 嫁)唔曾吖, 出門未呢。
11.	How many brothers have you?	你有幾多兄弟呢。
12.	One elder brother, one younger.	一個大佬, 一個細佬。
13.	Have you any sisters?	有姊妹冇呢。
14.	I have one elder sister and one younger.	一個亞姐, 一個亞妹。
15.	Are you married?	你娶老婆未曾呢。
16.	Not yet.	未曾(or 唔曾)娶咯。
17.	I cannot say certainly when I shall marry.	我唔話得定幾時娶親。
18.	My wife is in the house.	我女人(or 內人)喺屋踭。
19.	Oh! you will get married next year.	你出年娶老婆喇吓。
20.	Why is your child crying?	做乜你個細佬仔喊呢。
21.	He is hungry Perhaps he is thirsty as well.	佢肚餓囉；或者又係頸渴添。
22.	Give him something to eat, and to drink.	俾嘢佢食, 俾嘢佢飲囉。
23.	Call the nurse to carry him. Go with him for a walk.	叫奶媽嚟抱佢。去同佢行街。
24.	He is unwilling to come. Never mind whether he is willing or not.	佢唔肯嚟。唔打理佢肯唔肯。
25.	She has no husband; she is a widow.	[寡母婆。 佢冇老公(or 男人)嘅, 佢係
26.	A grandson and granddaughter live with her.	一個孫, 一個孫女同佢住。
27.	This is my nephew.	呢個係我姪叮。
28.	Is he a native of the place?	佢係本地人唔係呢。
29.	Why does he come here?	佢做乜嚟呢處呢。
30.	He has come to buy things for his grandfather.	佢嚟同亞公買嘢。
31.	When is he going back? Do you know?	佢幾時翻去呢。你知唔知呀。
32.	In two or three days with his cousin.	三兩日同表兄翻去囉。

LESSON VI.—Relationships.

1. ⌐Néí haí² mi ⌐yan* ⌐ni?²   You are what man, eh?53

2. ⌐K'öü haí² ⌐ngo ⌐lò-taú² lok⌐.   He is my father.39

3. ⌐Néí ⌐yaú ⌐lò-⌐mò⌐ ⌐mò ni?²   [⌐ni?²   You have mother, not, eh?53

4. ⌐Néí ⌐kéí * ⌐shí* ts'öü⌐ (or ts'öü³*)-⌐ts'an   You what time marry, eh?53

5. Shap₂ ⌐kéí ⌐nín. or shap₂ nín ⌐yaú ⌐to lo⌐.   Ten odd years, or ten years have more.31

6. ⌐Yaú ⌐tsaí ⌐nöü* (or ⌐nöü),⌐mò á⌐?   Have sons daughters, not, eh?2

7. ⌐Yaú ⌐kéí ko⌐ ⌐nöü*(or ⌐nöü), ⌐mò ⌐tsaí.   Have several [C.] daughters, no sons.
⌐⌐kéí táí⁵* ⌐ni?²   [eh?53

8. Chí⌐-táí² (or chí⌐-táí² ko⌐, or ke⌐) ⌐yaú   Greatest (or greatest C. or one) have how big

9. ⌐Kam ⌐nín ⌐yaú shap₂ ⌐kéí söü⌐.   This year have ten odd years.

10. Ká⌐-⌐cho(or ká³*) ⌐m ⌐ts'ang ⌐á?² Ch'ut, ⌐mún méí² ⌐ni?2   Married, not yet, eh?1 Gone-out-of doors, not-yet, eh?53.

11. ⌐Néí ⌐yaú ⌐kéí ⌐to ⌐hing-taí² ⌐ni?2   You have how many brothers, eh?53 [brother.

12. Yat, ko⌐ táí²-⌐lò, yat, ko⌐ saí⌐ ⌐lò.   One [C.] elder brother, one [C.] younger

13. ⌐Yaú ⌐tsz-möü² ⌐mò ni?2   [Á⌐-múí²).   Have sisters, not, eh?53

14. Yat, ko⌐ Á⌐-⌐tse, yat, ko⌐ Á⌐-múí³* (or   One [C.] elder-sister, one [C.] younger-sister.

15. ⌐Néí ts'öü³* (or ts'öü⌐) ⌐lò-⌐p'o méí² ts'ang, ⌐ni?2   [ts'öü³* lok⌐.   You married wife, not yet, eh?53

16. Méí² ⌐ts'ang, (or ⌐m ⌐ts'ang, or ⌐mengt)   Not yet (or not yet or not-yet) married.39

17. ⌐Ngo ⌐m wá² tak, ting² ⌐kéí ⌐shí* ts'öü³* (or ts'öü⌐) ⌐ts'an. 1   [⌐k'éí.   I not say can certain what time marry.

18. ⌐Ngo ⌐nöü ⌐yan* (or noí²-⌐yan) ⌐haí uk,-   My wife (lit. woman, or person within) in house.

19. ⌐Néí ch'ut, ⌐nín ts'öü³* (or ts'öü⌐) (often pronounced ⌐ts'ò) ⌐lò-⌐p'o lá.   [⌐ni?2   You coming year marry wife.21

20. Tsò²-mat, ⌐néí ko⌐ saí⌐-man-⌐tsaí hám⌐   Why your [C.] child cries, eh?53.

21. ⌐K'öü ⌐t'ò-ngo² lo⌐. Wák₂-⌐che yaú² haí² ⌐kengt-hot⌐ t'ím.   [⌐lo.   He hungry.31 Perhaps also is thirsty besides.

22. ⌐Péí ⌐ye ⌐k'öü shik, ⌐Péí ⌐ye ⌐k'öü ⌐yam   Give things him eat. Give thing him drink.30.

23. Kíú⌐ ⌐náí-⌐má ⌐laí ⌐p'ò ⌐k'öü. Höü⌐⌐t'ung ⌐k'öü ⌐hángt ⌐káí (or ⌐káí).   Call nurse come carry him. Go with him walk streets.

24. ⌐K'öü ⌐m ⌐hang ⌐laí. ⌐M ⌐tá-⌐leí ⌐k'öü ⌐hang ⌐m ⌐hang.   He not willing come Not mind he willing, not willing.

25. ⌐K'öü ⌐mò ⌐lò-⌐kung (or ⌐nám ⌐yan*) ke⌐; ⌐k'öü haí² ⌐kwá-⌐mò-⌐p'o.*   She no husband (or man) 15; she is widow. [her live.

26. Yat, ko⌐ ⌐sün, yat, ko⌐ ⌐sün-⌐nöü*(or ⌐sün ⌐nöü, but the other is better) ⌐t'ung ⌐k'öü   One [C.] grandson, one[C.] granddaughter with

27. Ni-ko⌐ haí² ⌐ngo chat₅* ⌐á.2   [chü².   This is my nephew.1

28. ⌐K'öü haí² ⌐pún-téí²-⌐yan ⌐m haí² ⌐ni?2   He is native, not is, eh?53

29. ⌐K'öü tsò²-mat, ⌐laí ni shü⌐ ⌐ni?2   He why comes this place, eh?53

30. ⌐K'öü ⌐laí ⌐t'ung Á⌐-⌐kung ⌐máí ⌐ye.   He comes for grandfather buy things.

31. ⌐K'öü ⌐kéí ⌐shí* fán höü⌐ ⌐ni? ⌐Néí ⌐chí ⌐m ⌐chí á⌐? [ary tone) ⌐fán höü⌐ lo⌐.   He what time back go, eh?53 You know, not know, eh?2 [back go.31

32. ⌐Sám ⌐löng yat₂ ⌐t'ung ⌐píú hing (or ordin-   Three two days with cousin (of different surname)

1. This is a more polite form than the above.

LESSON VII.—Opposites.

1.	This man is very tall and large.	呢個人好高大囉.
2.	I am shorter than he.	我矮過佢咯.
3.	That cow is fat.	嗰隻牛肥.
4.	This sheep is thin.	呢隻綿羊瘦.
5.	This string is too long.	呢條繩長過頭.
6.	The thread is too short; it is not enough.	呢條線短得嚀, 唔够使咯.
7.	This is a very large house. [on it.	呢間屋好大間囉.
8.	The road is so narrow you cannot walk	呢條路咁窄唔行得咯.
9.	This chair is strong.	呢張椅堅固.
10.	This table is very shaky.	呢張檯好浮.
11.	He is very strong.	佢身子好壯健.
12.	I am weaker than he.	我軟弱過佢.
13.	This table-cloth is wet.	呢張檯布濕.
14.	Dry it in the sun, and bring it back.	晒乾哩翻嚟喇.
15.	This rock is very hard.	呢礠石好硬.
16.	You must boil this meat till it is soft.	你要炶到呢的肉臉, *or* 呢的 肉你要炶到臉
17	Your hands are dirty [clean.	你對手污糟囉囉.
18.	It would be best for you to wash them	你去洗乾淨至好咯.
19.	I want hot water.	我要熱水.
20.	I do not want cold water.	唔要凍水呀.
21.	The sea is very deep. How deep is it?	大海好深呀. 有幾深呀.
22.	Rivers are more shallow than seas.	河淺過海.
23.	It is very far by water.	水路好遠咯.
24.	By land it is not as far by half	打路去冇一半咁遠.
25.	Those plaintains are not ripe yet.	嗰的蕉未熟咯.
26.	These coolie oranges are too unripe.	呢的橙生過頭.
27.	I don't want those eggs boiled so hard.	嗰的蛋唔好炶 (得) 咁老.
28.	I want to eat the oysters raw.	蠔我愛生食.
29.	There are a great many water-buffaloes.	有好多水牛.
30.	There are very few goats.	草羊好少呢.
31.	He is a very clever man.	佢係好聰明嘅人.
32.	You are very stupid.	你十分愚蠢咯.

---

1. This word may be omitted or not.

LESSON VII.—Opposites.

1.	Ni-ko' ⸢yan ⸢hò ⸢kò táí² po'.	This [C.] man very tall large.[60]
2.	⸤Ngo ⸢aí kwo' ⸤k·öü lok⸤.	I shorter than he.[53]
3.	⸢Ko˙ chek⸤ ⸤ngaú ⸤féí.	That [C.] cow fat.
4.	⸤Ni chek⸤ ⸤mín-⸤yöng˙ shaú'.	This [C.] sheep thin.
5.	⸤Ni ⸤t·íú ⸤shing˙ ⸤ch·öng-kwo³˙-⸤t·aú.	This piece string too-long.
6.	⸤Ni ⸤t·íú sin' ⸢tün-tak⸥-tsaí²; ⸤m kaú' ⸢shaí lok⸤.	This piece thread too-short ; not enough use.[32]
7.	⸤Ni ⸤kán uk⸥ ⸢hò táí² ⸤kán ká'.	This [C.] house very large one [or C.].[16]
8.	⸤Ni ⸤t·íú lò² kòm' chák⸤ ⸤m ⸤hángɫ tak⸥ lok⸤.	This length road so narrow not walk can.[32]
9.	⸤Ni ⸤chöng ⸢yí ⸤kín-kwú'.	This [C.] chair strong.
10.	⸤Ni ⸤chöng ⸤t·oí˙ ⸢hò ⸤faú.	This [C.] table very weak.
11.	⸤K·öü shan-⸢tsz ⸢hò chong'-kín².	His body very strong.
12.	⸤Ngo ⸤yün-yök⸥ kwo' ⸤k·öü.	I weaker than he.
13.	⸤Ni ⸤chöng ⸤t·oí˙-pò' shap⸥.	This [C.] table-cloth wet.
14.	Sháí' ⸤kon ⸤ning ⸤fán ⸤laí ⸤lá.²	Sun dry bring back come.[21]
15.	⸤Ni kaú² shek⸥ ⸢hò ngáng².	This piece rock very hard.
16.	⸤Néí yíú' sháp⸥ tò' ⸤ni· ti yuk⸥ ⸤nam, or ⸤Ni-⸤ti yuk⸥ ⸤néí yíú' sháp⸥ tò' ⸤nam.	You must boil until this meat tender, or This meat you must boil till tender.
17.	⸤Néí töü' ⸢shaú ⸤oᶜ-⸤tsò lo' po'.	Your pair-of hands dirty.[31] [21]
18.	⸤Néí hö̈ü' ⸢saí ⸤kon-tseng²ɫ chí'-⸢hò lok⸤.	You go wash clean best.[53]
19.	⸤Ngo yíú' yíɫ⸤ ⸢shöü.	I want hot water.
20.	⸤M yíú' tung ⸢shöü á'.	Not want cold water.
21.	Táí²-⸢hoí ⸢hò ⸤sham á'. ⸤Yaú ⸢kéí ⸤sham⸤	Great ocean very deep.² Have how deep.?²
22.	⸤Ho ⸢ts·ín kwo' ⸢hoí. [á'²?]	Rivers shallower than seas.
23.	⸢Shöü lò² ⸢hò ⸤yün lok⸤.	Water road very far.[32]
24.	⸢Tá lò² höü' ⸤mò yat⸥ pún' kòm' ⸤yün˙.	By road going not one half so far.
25.	Ko'-⸤ti tsíú méí² shuk⸥ lok⸤.	Those plantains not-yet ripe.[38]
26.	⸤Ni-⸤ti ⸤ch·áng˙ ⸤shángɫ kwo³˙-⸤t·aú.	These coolie-oranges unripe over-much (lit. over-head).
27.	Ko'-⸤ti tán³˙ ⸤m ⸢hò sháp⸥ (tak⸥) kòm' ⸤lò.	Those eggs not good boil (can) so old.
28.	⸤Hò, ⸤ngo oí' ⸤shángɫ shik⸥.	Oysters, I want raw eat.
29.	⸤Yaú ⸢hò ⸤to ⸢shöü-⸤ngaú. [chek⸤.	Have great many water-cows (or water-oxen).
30.	⸤Ts·ò-⸤yöng (or ⸢t·sò ⸤yöng˙) ⸢hò ⸢shíú	Goats very few.[7]
31.	⸤K·öü haí² ⸢hò ⸤ts·ung-⸤ming-ke' ⸤yan.	He is very clever's man.
32.	⸤Néí shap⸥ ⸤fan ⸤yü-⸢ch·un lokᵓ.	You ten parts stupid.[32]

---

1. Sometimes pronounced ú.

LESSON VIII.—Monetary.

1.	One dollar.	一個銀錢 (or)一文.
2.	A dollar and a half.	個半銀錢.
3.	Half a dollar.　Over a dollar.　[nounce.	半個銀錢. (or)半文. 個幾銀錢.
4.	This word 'ngan' is very difficult to pro-	呢個銀字好難講呀.
5.	Do you say so?　Do you pronounce it so?	你係噉話咩、你係噉講咩.
6.	That is easier to pronounce.　[pieces).	响個易啲講羅.
7.	A dollar is divided into ten 'ho,' (ten-cent	一個銀錢分十毫.
8.	One 'ho' is divided into ten cents.	一毫子分十仙.　　　　　毫六.
9.	Ten dollars and sixty-six cents. [dollars?	十個銀錢零六毫六、(or)十個六
10.	Can you change accounts in taels into	両數你唔伸元數唔唔呀.
11.	One tael is equal to a dollar and forty cents.	一両銀值得個四銀錢.
12.	Nine mace.　Nine cash.　[dollars to me.	九錢銀、九個錢.
13.	You agreed to hand over eighteen hundred	你應承交千八銀過我. '
14.	One tael, seven mace, six candareens, six léf.	一両七錢六分六.
15.	What is a dollar worth in cash?	一個銀錢找得幾多錢.
16.	It is worth one thousand and forty cash.	找得一千零四十錢.
17.	How much wages do you want a month?	你一個月要幾多人工呢.
18.	I want eight dollars a month.　This is too much.　　　[so much.	要八個銀錢個月、多過頭吁.
19.	My expenses are great, I cannot give you	我使費大、唔俾得咁多過你.
20.	If I find my own food, it is not much.	係食自己、唔係多吁.
21.	The master does not provide you with food; of course, you find yourself.	唔係食事頭、係食自已嘅定喇.
22.	I can't reduce my terms.　[done it.	唔滅得咯.
23.	Do you know how to do the work? I have	你曉做唔曉呀、我做過咯.
24.	You must not spend this money.	你唔好使呢啲錢.
25.	You ought to send it home.	你應該寄翻去歸.
26.	Does he gamble?　I think he does.	佢賭錢咩、我估係吁.
27.	Does he play at cards, or dominoes?	佢打乜野牌、紙牌嘥骨牌呢.
28.	Both; he also plays at fán-t'án, pò-tsz, and with dice.	両樣都有、又揸攤、打寶字、擲色.
29.	If he gambles, I shall not employ him.	佢係賭錢、我唔請佢.　(or 骰)
30.	You tell him.　I have.	你話佢聽、話咯.
31.	He says he won't dare do so.	佢話唔敢做咯.
32.	I take it he is acquainted with his work. Probably he is.	我睇得佢係熟手咯、大槪係呀.

1.　The 銀 in such a phrase is ambiguous: it may mean dollars, or taels.

LESSON VIII.—Monetary.

1.	Yat⟩ ko⟩ ꜀ngan ₋ts'ín,* *or* yat⟩ ₒman.	One [C.] silver cash, *or* one dollar.
2.	Ko⟩ pún⟩ ꜀ngan-₋ts'ín* [꜀kéí ꜀ngan-₋ts'ín.*	One (*and a*) half dollar. [dollar.
3.	Pún⟩ ko⟩ ꜀ngan-₋ts'ín,* *or* pún⟩ ₒman. Ko⟩	Half [C.] dollar, *or* half dollar. One (*and*) odd
4.	꜀Ni-ko⟩ ꜀ngan tsz² ꜀hò ꜀nán ꜀kong á⟩	This *ngan* character very difficult to-speak. ²
5.	꜄Néí haí² ꜀kòm wá² ₋me?² ꜄Néí haí² ꜀kòm ꜀kong ₋me?²	You do so say, do-you? ³⁹ You do so say (*or* pronounce), eh? ³⁹
6.	꜀Ko-ko⟩ yí²-₋ti ꜀kong lo⟩.	That easier to-say (*or* pronounce).³¹
7.	Yat⟩ ko⟩ ꜀ngan-₋ts'ín* ꜀fan shap₂ ₋hò.	One [C.] dollar divided ten dimes.
8.	Yat⟩ ꜀hò-꜄tsz ꜀fan shap₂ ₒsín.	One dime divided ten cents.
9.	Shap₂ ko⟩ ꜀ngan-₋ts'ín* ꜀lengt luk₂ ₋hò luk₂, *or* shap₂ ko⟩ luk₂ ꜀hò luk₂.	Ten [C.] dollars and six dime six (*cents*), *or* ten [C.] six dimes six.
10.	꜀Lŏng shò⟩ ꜄néí ꜄wúí ꜀shan ꜀yün shò⟩, ₋m ꜄wúí á⟩? [₋ts'ín*.	Tael accounts you can carry-out-into dollar accounts, not can, eh?²
11.	Yat⟩ ꜀lŏng ngan chik₂-tak⟩ ko⟩ sz⟩ ꜀ngan-	One tael silver worth one [*or* C.] four dollar. ·
12.	꜀Kaú ₋ts'ín ꜀ngan. ꜀Kaú ko⟩ ₋ts'ín*.	Nine mace silver. Nine [C.] cash.
13.	꜄Néí ꜀ying-꜀shing ꜀káú ₋ts'ín pát₀ ꜀ngan kwo⟩ ꜄ngo.	You agreed hand-over thousand eight money to me.
14.	Yat⟩ ꜀lŏng ts'at₂ ₋ts'ín luk₂ ꜀fan luk₂.	One tael seven mace six candareens six (*léí*).
15.	Yat⟩ ko⟩ ꜀ngan-₋ts'ín* ꜀cháú tak⟩ ꜀kéí ₀to ₋ts'ín*? [₋ts'ín.	One [C.] dollar change can how many cash?
16.	꜀Cháú tak⟩ yat⟩ ₋ts'ín ꜀lengt sz⟩-shap₂	Change can one thousand and forty cash.
17.	꜄Néí yat⟩ ko⟩ yüt₂ yíú⟩ ꜀kéí₀to ꜀yan-꜀kung ni?² [kwo⟩•-₋t'aú ₋á.²	You one [C.] month want how much wages, eh?⁵³
18.	Yíú⟩ pát₀ ko⟩ ꜀ngan-₋ts'ín* ko⟩ yüt₂. To	Want eight [C.] dollars [C.] month. Much too.¹
19.	꜄Ngo ꜀shaí-faí⟩ táí²; ₋m ꜀péí tak⟩ kòm⟩ ₋to kwo⟩ ꜄néí.	My expenses great; not give able so much to you.
20.	Haí² shik₂ tsz²-꜀kéí, ₋m haí² ₋to ₋á.²	Do eat self, not is much.¹
21.	₋M haí² shik₂ ₋sz²-꜀t'aú,* haí² shik₂ tsz²-꜀kéí-ke⟩ ting꜄•꜀lá.²	Not do eat master, do eat self's certainly.²¹
22.	₋M ꜀kám tak⟩ lok₀. [lok₀.	Not reduce can.³²
23.	꜄Néí ꜀híú tsò⟩ ₋m ꜀híú á⟩? ꜄Ngo tsò² kwo⟩	You know do, not know, eh?² I done already.³²
24.	꜄Néí ₋m ꜀hò ꜀shaí ni-₋ti ₋ts'ín.*	You not good use this money.
25.	꜄Néí ꜀ying-꜀koí kéí⟩ ꜀fán höü⟩ kwaí. [₋á.²	You ought send back go home.
26.	꜄K'öü ꜀tò-₋ts'ín* ₋me?² ꜄Ngo ꜀kwú haí²	He gamble, eh?³⁹ I think does.¹
27.	꜄K'öü ꜀tá mat₂-꜄ye ₋p'áí*, ꜀chí ₋p'áí* péí² kwat₂ ₋p'áí* ni?²	He play-at what, dominoes-or-cards, paper cards, or bone tablets, eh?⁵³
28.	꜄Lŏng yŏng² ₋tò ꜄yaú; yaú² ꜀chá ₋t'án, ꜀tá ꜀pò-tsz꜄•, chák₂ shik₂. [꜄k'öü.	Two kinds also have; further play-at fán-t'án, play-at pò-tsz, throw dice.
29.	꜄K'öü haí² ꜀tò-₋ts'ín* ꜄ngo ₋m ꜀ts'engt	He does gamble, I not engage him.
30.	꜄Néí wá² ꜄k'öü ꜀t'eng.t Wá꜄• lok₀.	You tell him to-hear. Told.³²
31.	꜄K'öü wá² ₋m ꜀kòm tsò² lok₀.	He says not dare do.³²
32.	꜄Ngo ꜀t'aí-tak⟩ ꜄k'öü haí² shuk₂ ꜀shaú lok₀. Táí²-k'oí꜄• haí² á⟩.	I see-can he is acquainted 'hand.'³² Probably is.²

LESSON IX.—Commercial.

1.	How much is this?	呢啲幾多銀 (*or* 錢) 呢。
2.	What is the price of that?	個啲幾多價錢呢。
3.	It is too dear.	賞過頭、*or* 賞得滯咯。
4.	I shall not buy it. I don't want it.	我唔買呀、唔要咯。
5.	Have you any cheaper ones?	有平啲嘅冇呀。
6.	This is cheaper.	呢個平啲啊。
7	How do you sell this rice? [prices.	呢啲米點賣呢。
8.	Oh! don't stand out so. Reduce your	唉吔、麻麻哋、減價喇。
9.	Increase your offer. You are dear.	你添啲喇、 你賞咗。
10.	No. They are first quality of goods.	唔係賞咗、係第一好貨咯。
11.	Is it good? Mine are the best.	好唔好咗、我嘅至好咯。
12.	I saw better ones before.	我舊時見過好啲嘅。
13.	Have you any better ones?	重有好啲嘅冇呢。
14.	Bring them for me to see.	掉嚟俾我睇。
15.	If suitable, I shall certainly buy.	合使、我是必買咗。
16.	It does not matter if they are dearer.	賞的、都唔計帶咗。
17.	There are none as good as these through-out Hongkong.	通香港都冇呢啲咁好嘅。
18.	It is imitation. No; it is genuine.	係假嘅、唔係係真嘅。
19.	You don't know that these are good things.	你都唔分得開貴賤嘅咯。
20.	I do. I have been in that business. Indeed!	識咗、我都做過個啲生意咯、係。
21.	I am afraid it is old, is it not? No, it is new.	係舊嘅嘛呼、唔係、係新嘅。
22.	This is no use. It is useless.	呢個冇用、唔中用咯。
23.	He wants too high a price.	佢要得價錢多。
24.	You offer too little. Don't be so stingy.	你俾得少咗、唔好留住價咗。
25.	It will not pay cost price.	唔够本(*or* 本錢) 咗。
26.	How long will it last?	使得幾耐呢。
27.	I guarantee it will last four years.	我包可以用得四年。
28.	That is a promissory note, is it?	個張係揭單咩。
29.	How much is the capital and interest?	本銀利息*or simply* 本利, *or* 本息) 幾多呀。
30.	The interest is only three dollars per men-sem. [rather little interest.	每月三個銀錢利息啫。
31.	That's very heavy interest. No; it is	好重利呀、唔係咗、幾平利呀。
32.	The capital is one hundred dollars payable on demand.	本銀一百元隨時取囘。

LESSON IX.—Commercial.

1. ‿Ni-‿ti ⸢kéí ‿to ‿ngan* (or ‿ts'ín*)[1] ‿ni ?[2].	This how much money (or cash), eh ?[53]
2. Ko⸣-‿oti ⸢kéí ‿to ká⸣-‿ts'ín ‿ni ?[2]	That how much price, eh ?[53]
3. Kwaí⸣ kwo²*‿t'aú, or kwaí⸣ tak‿-tsaí² lok‿o.	Dear over much, or dear much-too.[32]
4. ⸢Ngo ‿m ⸢máí á⸣. ‿M yíú⸣ lok‿o.	I not buy.[2] Not want.[32]
5. ⸢Yaú ‿p'eng-† ‿ti ke⸣ ⸢mò á⸣ ?	Have cheaper ones not, eh ?[2]
6. ‿Ni-ko⸣ ‿p'eng†‿ ‿ti o⸣ ?	This cheaper.[56]
7. ‿Ni-‿ti ⸢maí ⸢tím máí² ‿ni ?[2] ‿[ká⸣ ‿lá.[2]	This rice how sell, eh ?[53]
8. ‿Ai-‿yá, (or ‿Ai-‿yá) ‿má-‿má*-téí⸣*, ⸢Kám	Oh ! let-it-pass. Reduce price.[21]
9. ⸢Néí ‿t'ím ‿ti lá.[2] ⸢Néí kwaí⸣ ‿á.[2] ‿[lok‿o.	You increase little.[21] You dear.[1]
10. ‿M haí² kwaí⸣ ‿á.[2] Haí² taí² yat‿ ⸢hò ſo⸣	Not is dear.[1] Are No. 1 good articles.[32]
11. ⸢Hò ‿m ⸢hò ‿á ?[2] ⸢Ngo-ke⸣ chí⸣-⸢hò lok‿o.	Good not good eh ?[1] Mine best.[32]
12. ⸢Ngo kaú² ‿shí* kín⸣-kwo⸣ ⸢hò-‿ti ke⸣.	I old time (formerly) seen have better ones.
13. Chung² ⸢yaú ⸢hò-‿ti ke⸣ ⸢mò ‿ni ?[2]	Besides have better-ones, not, eh ?[53]
14. ‿Ning ‿laí ⸢péí ⸢ngo ⸢t'aí.	Bring come give me see.
15. Hòp‿ɔ ⸢shaí, ⸢ngo shí²-pít, ⸢máí ‿á.[2]	Suitable for-use, I certainly buy.[1]
16. Kwaí⸣-‿ti tò ‿m kaí⸣ táí⸣ ‿á.[2] ‿[⸢hò ke⸣.	Dearer even not reckon-it (or no matter).[1]
17. ‿T'ung* ‿Höng-⸢kong tò ⸢mò ‿ni-‿ti kòm⸣.	Throughout Hongkong even not these so good.[15]
18. Haí² ⸢ká ke⸣. ‿M haí² ; haí² ‿chan ke⸣.	Is false.[15] Not is ; is true.[15]
19. ⸢Níé ‿tò ‿m ‿fan-tak‿,-⸢hoí kwaí⸣ tsín² ke⸣ lok‿o.	You even not divide-able-out valuable vile.[15,32].
20. Shik‿ ‿á.[2] ⸢Ngo ‿tò tsò⸣ kwo⸣ ‿ko-‿ti sháng† yí⸣ lok‿o. Haí⸣* ? ‿[‿san ke⸣.	Know.[1] I also done over that business.[32] Indeed? [Notice this is changed into a variant tone.]
21. Haí² kaú² ke⸣ lá⸣ kwá⸣ ? ‿M haí², háí²	Is old one,[21] probably-'tis-isn't-it ?[18] Not is, is
22. ‿Ni-ko⸣ ⸢mò yung². ‿M-‿chung-yung² lok‿o.	This no use. Useless.[32] [new.[15]
23. ⸢K'öü yíú⸣-tak‿ ká⸣-‿ts'ín ‿to.	He wants price much.
24. ⸢Néí ⸢péí-tak‿ ⸢shíú ‿á.[2] ‿M ⸢hò ‿laú-chü²-ká⸣ ‿á (or ‿á).	You offer little.[1] Not good to-hold-the-price-in.[1] [cost-money.)[1]
25. ‿M kaú⸣ ⸢pún (or ⸢pún ‿ts'ín) ‿á.[2]	Not enough (to equal) cost-price[1], (or original
26. ⸢Shaí tak‿ ⸢kéí noí⸣,* ‿ni ?[2]	Use can how long, eh ?[53]
27. ⸢Ngo ‿paú (⸢ho-⸢yí) yung² tak‿ sz⸣ ‿nín.	I guarantee (able) use can four years.
28. ⸢Ko ‿chöng haí² k'ít‿ ‿tán ‿me ?[2]	That [C.] is promissory note, is-it ?[39]
29. ⸢Pún ‿ngan, léí²-‿sik‿ (or simply ⸢pún léí², or ⸢pún sik‿) ⸢kéí ‿to á⸣ ? ‿[che.	Capital money, interest (or principal interest), how much, eh ?[1]
30. ⸢Múí yüt‿ɔ ⸢sám ko⸣ ‿ngan-‿ts'ín* léí²-‿sik‿	Each month three [C.] dollars interest only.[8]
31. ⸢Hò ⸢ch'ung léí² á⸣. ‿M haí² ‿á ; ⸢kéí ‿p'eng† léí² á⸣.	Very heavy interest.[2] Not is ;[1] rather cheap interest.[2]
32. ⸢Pún ‿ngan yat‿ pák‿ɔ ‿yün, ‿ts'öü ‿shí ⸢ts'öü ‿wúí.	Capital money one hundred dollars, any time take back.

---

1. Use the *former* if the price is likely to be given in silver, and the latter if in cash.

LESSON X.—Commercial.

1.	What business does he carry on ?	佢做乜野生意呢.
2.	I am a general merchant.	我做南北行嘅.
3.	Where is your hong ?	你間行喺邊處呀.
4.	What is it called *(its style)* ?	乜野字號呢.
5.	How long have you been in business ?	你做生意有幾耐呀.
6.	Call the compradore first though.	叫買辦嚟喳.
7.	Have you made up your accounts ?	你計數唔曾呀.
8.	I have not made them up completely yet.	唔曾計清楚咯.
9.	Compare accounts with me.	同我對數喇.
10.	Wait a bit, this item is wrong.	等吓咋、呢條錯咯.
11.	It must be gone over again. That will do.	要計過咯、做得羅.
12.	Has that money been shroffed ?	睇過個啲銀唔曾呀.
13.	Call the shroff to shroff it. [changed.	叫睇銀嘅嚟睇喇.
14.	If there are any bad ones, they must be	有唔好嘅要換瞞.
15.	Weigh these dollars. [light.	兌呢啲銀喇.
16.	Ten of them are not full weight ; they are	十個唔够重呀、輕叮.
17.	Who is the accountant here ?	呢處邊個做掌櫃呢.
18.	My friend. This is the manager.	我朋友、呢個係做司事人.
19.	Has he a share in the business ?	生意佢有份冇呀.
20.	What goods are these ?	呢啲係乜野貨呢.
21.	All miscellaneous goods.	喊啡吟都係雜貨咯.
22.	Have they passed the Customs ? [Lading ?	過稅唔曾呢.
23.	They have passed. Where is the Bill of	過咽咯、攬載紙呢.
24.	He wants to open a shop. [capital)	佢想開間舖.
25.	I am afraid he will lose his money *(lit.*	我慌佢賒本呀.
26.	Where is his shop ? [very dull.	佢個間舖喺邊處呢.
27.	There is not much business here. It is	呢處冇乜生意呀、好淡叮.
28.	What were the good-will, stock-in-trade and fittings sold for ? [to him, was it ?	招牌、舖底、傢生頂得幾多銀呢.
29.	Then it was you that sold that business	噉、個啲生意係你頂過佢咩.
30.	Call men to carry the goods into the go-down. I will not come to-morrow, as it is Sunday.	叫人抬貨落貨倉喇. 聽日禮拜我唔嚟咯.
31.	When does the steamer leave ? There are a great many passengers.	火船幾時開身呢、 有大多搭客咯.
32.	I want to send some letters *(or* a letter) home to the country.	我要寄信翻去歸鄉下.

LESSON X.—Commercial.

1.	ᶜK'òū tsò² mi ᶜye ᵍshángꬷ-yí⁾ ᶜni⁾ ? ²	He does what thing business, eh ?⁵³
2.	ᶜNgo tsò² ᵧnám-pak, ᵧhong⁾ keˢ.	I do south-north hong's.¹⁵
3.	ᶜNéí ᵧkán ᵧhong⁾ ᶜhaí ₒpín shü⁾ á⁾ ?	Your [C.] hong at what place, eh ?²
4.	ᵧMi ᶜye tsz²-hò² ᵧni ? ²	What (thing) style, eh ?⁵³
5.	ᶜNéí tsò² ᵧshángꬷ-yí⁾ ᶜyaú ᶜkéí noí⁵⁺ á⁾ ?	You do business have how long, eh ?²
6.	Kíú⁾ ᶜmáí-pán⁵⁺ ᵧlaí ᶜchá.	Call compradore come first.⁵
7.	ᶜNéí kaí³⁺ shò⁾ ᵧm ᵧts'ang á⁾ ?	You reckon accounts not yet, eh ?²
8.	ᵧM ᵧts'ang kaí⁾ ᵧts'ing-ᶜch'o lokₒ.	Not yet reckoned clearly.³²
9.	ᵧT'ung ᶜngo töū⁾ shò⁾ ᵧlá.²	With me compare accounts. ²¹
10.	ᶜTang ᶜhá chá⁾, ᵧni ᵧt'íú ts'o⁾ lokₒ.	Wait bit first,⁶ this item wrong.³²
11.	Yíú⁾ kaí⁾ kwo⁾ lokₒ. Tsò² tak, lo⁾.	Must reckon again.³² Do can.³¹
12.	ᶜT'aí kwo⁾ ko⁾-ₒti ᵧngan⁺ ᵧm ᵧts'ang á⁾ ?	Looked over that money not yet, eh ?²
13.	Kíú⁾ ᶜt'aí-ᵧngan⁺-ke⁾ ᵧlaí ᶜt'aí ᵧlá.²	Call shroffing-one come look. ²¹
14.	ᶜYaú ᵧm ᶜhò ke⁾ yíú⁾ wún² po⁾.	Have not good ones must change.⁶⁰
15.	Töū⁾ ᵧni-ₜti ᵧngan⁺ lá ²	Weigh these dollars. ²¹
16.	Shap₂ ko⁾ ᵧm kaú⁾ ᶜch'ung ꬷ á⁾. ᵧHengꬷ á.²	Ten [C.] not enough heavy.² Light.¹
17.	Ni-shü⁾ ₒpín ko⁾ tsò² ᶜchöng-kwaí⁵⁺ ᵧni ?²	This-place who [C.] is accountant, eh ?⁵³
18.	ᶜNgo ᵧp'ang-ᶜyaú. ᵧNi-ko⁾ haí⁾ tsò² ᵧsz-sz²-ᵧyan.	My friend. This [C.] is being manager.
19.	ᵧShángꬷ-yí⁾ ᶜk'öū ᶜyaú fan⁵⁺ ᶜmò á⁾ ?	Business he has share, not, eh ?²
20.	ᵧNi-ₜti haí² mi ᶜye fo⁾ ᵧni ? ²	These are what thing goods, eh ?⁵³
21.	Hám²-pá²-láng² ₒtò haí² tsáp₂ fo⁾ lokₒ.	All even are miscellaneous goods.³²
22.	Kwo³⁺ shöū⁾ ᵧm ᵧts'ang ni ? ²	Passed customs not yet, eh ?⁵³
23.	Kwo⁾ ᶜcho lokₒ. ᶜLám-tsoí⁾-ᶜchí ᵧni ? ²	Passed [s. of p. t.].³² Bill-of-Lading, eh ?⁵³
24.	ᶜK'öū ᶜsöng ᵧhoí ᵧkán p'ò⁾.	He wishes open [C.] shop.
25.	ᶜNgo ᵧfong ᶜk'öū shít₂ ᶜpún á⁾.	I fear he lose capital.² [place, eh ?⁵³
26.	ᶜK'öū ᶜko ᵧkán p'ò⁾ ᶜhaí ₒpín shü⁾ ᵧni ?²	His that [C.] shop (that shop of his) at what
27.	ᵧNi shü⁾ ᶜmò mat, ᵧshángꬷ-yí⁾ á⁾. ᶜHò tám² á.²	This place not much business.² Very dull.¹
28.	ᵧChíú-ᵧp'áí, p'ò⁾-ᶜtaí, ká⁾-ᵧshángꬷ ᶜting tak, ᶜkéí ₒto ᵧngan⁺ ᵧni ? ²	Signboard, shop-residue, furniture, sold able how much money, eh ?⁵³
29.	ᶜKòm₂, ᵧko-ₒti ᵧshángꬷ-yí⁾ haí² ᶜnéí ᶜting kwo⁾ ᶜk'öū ᵧme ?²	Then that business 'twas you sold (it) to him, was it ?³⁹
30.	Kíú⁾ ᵧyan ᵧt'oí fo⁾ lokₒ, fo⁾-ᵧts'ong ᵧlá.² ᵧT'ing (or ₒT'ing)-yat₂ ᶜLaí-pái⁾ ᶜngo ᵧm ᵧlaí lokₒ.	Call men carry goods down go-down.²¹ To-morrow, Sunday, I not come.⁶²
31.	ᶜFo-ᵧshün ᶜkéí ᵧshí⁺ ᵧhoí-ᵧshan ᵧni ?² ᶜYaú táí² ₒto táp -hák lok .	Steamer what time start, eh ?⁵³ Have great many passengers.³²
32.	ᶜNgo yíú⁾ kéí⁾ sun⁾ ᵧfán höū⁾ ᵧkwaí ᵧhöng-ᶜhá.	I want send letter back go home country.

LESSON XI.—Medical.

1.	This gentleman is a doctor.	呢位係醫生咯。
2.	Is he a surgeon, or physician?	佢係外科醫生、嗰內科呢。
3.	Call a Chinese doctor to feel my pulse.	請唐人醫生嚟睇脈呀。
4.	I am not very well to-day.	我今日唔多自然咯。
5.	What is the matter with you?	你有乜野病呢。
6.	My head aches.	頭痢呀。
7.	Have you been sick?	有嘔冇呢。
8.	I have not, but I feel inclined to be so.	冇嘔、想嘔哦。
9.	Is there anything else the matter?	重有乜野病冇呢。
10.	I have also the stomach-ache.	我肚都痛吖。
11.	That is not serious.	個啲冇乜相干嚹。
12.	Take a little medicine.	食啲藥喇。
13.	What medicine ought I to take?	我應食乜野藥呢。
14.	Wait till I come back. I am going to the hospital now.	等我翻黎咋、我而家去醫生館。
15.	I will send a man with medicine for you.	我打發人捽藥嚟俾你。
16.	You have fever. I will give you a draught.	你發熱羅、我俾藥水你食。
17.	I have ague. Take this powder.	我發冷羅、食呢啲藥散。
18.	Do you feel your throat dry?	你見喉嚨乾咩。
19.	I do, and it is very painful.	見乾羅、又見好痛添咯。
20.	Don't drink so much water.	咪飲咁多水吖。
21.	Take a little chicken broth. Take a little congee.	飲啲鷄湯、食啲粥吖。
22	Are you able to sleep at night?	瞓頭瞓得、唔瞓得呢。
23.	Has he got cold? Does he cough?	佢冷親咩、佢咳嗎。
24.	At times he does, at times he doesn't.	有時有、有時冇。
25.	Put on a plaster. Does he drink?	貼膏藥、佢飲酒唔飲呀。
26.	I am afraid he smokes opium.	我慌佢食鴉片煙嘅。
27.	Perhaps he does. I am afraid he does.	怕係呀、或者係都唔定呀。
28.	How long has he been ill?	佢病有幾耐呢。
29.	He has been feeling weak for a long time.	佢好耐見軟弱羅。
30.	Tell him to take some cooling medicine.	叫佢食啲涼藥喇。
31.	Did he feel better after taking the pills?	佢食嗰藥丸見好啲嗎。
32.	No, he was much worse..	唔係、越發敝咯。

---

1 飲 ʽYam could be used; but the above form is better.

LESSON XI.—Medical.

1. ꞔNi waí⁵• haí² ꞔyí-ₒsháng† (or ꞔyí-ₒshang) lokₒ.	This [C.] is doctor. ³²
2. ꞔK·öü haí² ngoí²-ꞔfo ꞔyí-ₒshángt, (or short a) péí² noí²-ꞔfo ꞔni ?²	He is external-practice doctor, or internal-practice, eh ?⁵³
3. ꞔTs·engt ꞔT·ong-ꞔyan ꞔyí-ₒshángt (or short a) ꞔlaí ꞔt·aí mak₂ á⁵.	Invite Chinese doctor come feel pulse. ⁸
4. ꞔNgo ꞔkam-yat₂ ꞔm ₒto tsz²-ꞔyín lokₒ.	I to-day not very well. ³²
5. ꞔNéí ꞔyaú mat₂-ꞔye peng²† ꞔni ?	You have what-thing sickness, eh ? ⁵³
6. ꞔT·aú-ts·ek † á⁵.	Headache. ²
7. ꞔYaú ꞔaú ꞔmò ꞔni ?²	Have sick not, eh ? ⁵³
8. ꞔMò꞊ᵗaú ; ꞔsŏng ꞔaú ꞔche.²	Not sick ; wish to-be-sick only. ⁷
9. Chung² ꞔyaú ꞔmi-ꞔye peng²† ꞔmò ꞔni ?²	Besides have what sickness not, eh ? ⁵³
10. ꞔNgo ꞔt·ò ₒtò t·ung⁵ ꞔá.²	My stomach also pains. ¹
11. Ko⁵-ₒti ꞔmò mat₂ ꞔsŏng-ꞔkòn ká⁵.	That not much matter. ¹⁴
12. Shik₂ ₒti yŏk₂ ꞔlá.²	Eat some medicine. ²¹
13. ꞔNgo ꞔying shik₂ ꞔmi-ꞔye yŏk₂ ꞔni ?²	I ought to-eat what medicine, eh ? ⁵³
14. ꞔTang ꞔngo ꞔfán ꞔlaí chá⁵. ꞔNgo ꞔyí-ₒká höü⁵ ꞔyí-ₒsháng-(or short a) ꞔkwún.	Wait I back come until.⁶ I at-present go hospital.
15. ꞔNgo ꞔtá-fát₀ꞔyan ꞔning yŏk₂ ꞔlaí ꞔpéí ꞔnéí.	I send man bring medicine come give you.
16. ꞔNéí fát₀-yít₂ lo⁵. ꞔNgo ꞔpéí yŏk₂ ꞔshöü ꞔnéí shik₂. [ꞔsán.	You have-fever.³¹ I give medicine water (i.e., liquid medicine) you eat.
17. ꞔNgo fát₀-ꞔláng lo⁵. Shik₂ ꞔni-ₒti yŏk₂	I have-ague.³¹ Eat this medicine powder.
18. ꞔNéí kín⁵ ꞔhaú-ꞔlung ꞔkon me ?²	You feel throat dry, eh ? ³⁹
19. Kín⁵ ꞔkon lo⁵ ; yaú² kín⁵ ꞔhò t·ung⁵ t·ím lokₒ.	Feel dry ;³¹ also feel very painful besides. ³²
20. ꞔMaí ꞔyam kòm⁵ ꞔto ꞔshöü ꞔá.²	Don't drink so much water. ¹
21. ꞔYam ₒti ꞔkaí t·ong ; shik₂ ₒti chuk₂ ꞔá. ²	Drink some chicken soup ; eat some congee. ¹
22. ꞔMán-ꞔt·aú• fan₂-tak₂, ꞔm fan²-tak₂ ꞔni ?²	Night-time sleep-can, not sleep-can, eh ? ⁵³
23. ꞔK·öü ꞔláng-ꞔts·an me ? ꞔK·öü k·at₂ ꞔmá ?	He cold-caught, eh ? ³⁹ He cough, eh ? ³⁷
24. ꞔYaú ꞔshí• (or ꞔshí) ꞔyaú ; ꞔyaú ꞔshí• (or ꞔshí) ꞔmò.	Have times have ; have times not.
25. T·íp₀ ꞔkò-yŏk₂. ꞔK·öü ꞔyam ꞔtsaú, ꞔm ꞔyam á⁵ ?	Stick-on plaster. He drink wine, not drink, eh ?²
26. ꞔNgo ꞔfong ꞔk·öü shik₂ á-p·ín⁵-ₒyín ke⁵.	I fear he smokes opium. ¹⁵
27. P·á⁵ haí² á⁵ Wák₂-ꞔche haí² ₒtò ꞔm ting² á².	Fear does. ² Perhaps does also not certain. ³
28. ꞔK·öü peng²† (or peng⁵•) ꞔyaú ꞔkéí noí⁵• ꞔni ? ²	He ill have how long, eh ? ⁵³
29. ꞔK·öü ꞔhò noí² kín⁵ ꞔyün-yŏk₂ lo⁵.	He very long feel weak. ³¹
30. Kíú⁵ ꞔk·öü shik₀ₒti ꞔlŏng yŏk₂ ꞔlá. ²	Tell him eat some cooling medicine. ²¹
31. ꞔK·öü shik₂-ꞔcho yŏk₂-ꞔyün• kín⁵ ꞔhò-ₒti	He eat [s. of p. t.] pills feel better, eh ? ³⁷
32. ꞔM haí², yüt₂-fát₀ paí² lokₒ. [ꞔmá ?²	Not is, the-rather the-worse.³²

LESSON XII.—Ecclesiastical.

1.	Is this a convent or not?	呢間係庵唔係呢。
2.	Are there any priests?	有和尚冇呀。
3.	There are no priests; there are nuns only.	冇和尚、有尼姑啫。
4.	How many are there?　Are there many or few?	有幾多個呢、多嘝少呢。
5.	Over twenty.　Twenty and more.	二十零個、二十個有多咯。
6.	What do they, the priests, do?	佢哋呢、和尚呢、做乜野呢。
7.	Read the Sutras the whole day long, so they say.	成日念經啊。
8.	Do you believe it?　No one does.	你信唔信吖、冇人信嘅。
9.	That is a temple.　I do not know whether it is a Buddhist, or Taoist one.	個間係廟、唔知係佛教嘅。嘝道教嘅呢。
10.	It is a Buddhist temple.	係佛教嘅。
11.	What is the difference?	有乜分別呢。
12.	There is a great difference.	有大分別咯、or 大有分別咯。
13.	What idols are those?	個的係乜野菩薩呢。
14.	The three Precious Buddhas.	係三寶佛咯。
15.	He is a Protestant missionary.	佢係講耶穌嘅。
16.	Have you become a convert?　I have not.	你入教唔曾呀、未曾呀。
17.	Why have you not?	做乜你唔曾入教嘅咩。
18.	Is there a chapel here?	呢處有禮拜堂冇呢。
19.	There are two; and there is someone preaching every day.	有兩間咯、日日有人講書。
20.	Are they Protestant or Catholic?	係天主教嘅、嘝耶穌教嘅呢。
21.	One is Protestant.	一間係耶穌教嘅。
22.	One (or The other) is Catholic	一(or 個)間係天主教嘅。
23.	Who are the Catholic Missionaries?	神父係乜人呀。
24.	They are all Frenchmen.	個個都係法蘭西人呀。
25.	Have they families?	佢哋有家眷冇呢。
26.	They are not allowed to marry.	唔准佢娶老婆嘅。
27.	They wear Chinese clothes.	佢扮唐裝嘅咯。
28.	What is the intention in this?	有乜意思呢。
29.	They want to be like Chinese.	佢想學翻唐人一樣。
30.	Is there any other reason?	重有乜緣故冇呢。
31.	You must ask them to know.	要問佢就知囉。
32.	I am a Chinese, and do not know.	我係唐人、唔知到吖。

LESSON XII.—Ecclesiastical.

1. Ni ‚kán haí² ‚òm ‚m haí² ‚ni ? ²	This [C.] is convent not is, eh ? ⁵³
2. ⁵Yaú ‚wo-shöng³ᵉ ⁵mò á² ?	Have (Buddhist) priests (or) not, eh ? ²
3. ⁵Mò ‚wo-shöng³ᵉ ; ⁵yaú ‚néí-‚kwú ‚che.²	No (Buddhist) priests ; have nuns only. ⁷
4. ⁵Yaú ⁵kéí ‚to ko² ‚ni ? ‚To pé² ⁵shíú ‚ni? ²	Have how many [C.], eh ?⁵³ Many or few, eh ?⁵³
5. Yí²-shap₂ ‚lengt ko³ᵉ Yí² shap₂ ko² ⁵yaú ‚to lok ‚ (or only Yí² shap₂ ko²).	Twenty odd [C.]. Twenty [C.] have more. ³²
6. ⁵K‘öü-téí² ‚ni, ‚wo-shöng³ᵉ ‚ni, tsò² ‚mi-⁵ye ‚ni? ²	They, ⁵³ priests, ⁵³ do what thing, eh ? ⁵³
7. ‚Shengt yat₂ ním²-‚king ⁵wo.	Whole day recite-sutras, (so they) say. ⁶⁵
8. ⁵Néí sun² ‚m sun² á? ⁵Mò ‚yan sun²ke².	You believe not believe, eh ?¹ No man believes. ¹⁵
9. Ko² ‚kán haí² míú³ᵉ. ‚M ‚chí haí² Fat₂-káú² ke², pé² Tò²-káú²-ke² ‚ni. ²	That [C.] is temple. Not know is Buddhist-sect's, ¹⁵ or Taouist-sect's ?¹⁵ ⁵³
10. Haí² Fat₂-káú² ke².	Is Buddhist-sect's. ¹⁵
11. ⁵Yaú mat, ‚fan-pít₂ ‚ni ? ²	Have what difference, eh ? ⁵³
12. ⁵Yaú táí² ‚fan-pít₂ lok‚. or táí² ⁵yaú ‚fan-pít₂ lok‚	Have great difference, ³² or great have difference. ³²
13. Ko²-‚ti haí² mat,-⁵ye ‚p‘ò-sát ‚ni ?	Those are what idols, eh ? ⁵³
14. Haí² ‚Sám ⁵Pò Fat₂ lok‚.	Are Three Precious Buddhas. ³²
15. ⁵K‘öü haí² ⁵kong ‚Ye-‚sò ke².	He is speak Jesus'? ¹⁵
16. ⁵Néí yap₂ káú² ‚m-‚ts'ang á²? Meí²-‚ts'ang á². [‚me ? ²	You entered the-faith not-yet, eh? ² Not yet. ²
17. Tsò² mat, ⁵néí ‚m ‚ts'ang yap₂ káú² ke²	What thing you not yet entered the-faith, eh ?¹⁵ ³⁹
18. Ni-shü² ⁵yaú ⁵Laí-páí² ‚t'ong ⁵mò ‚ni? ²	This-place have Sabbath Hall not, eh ? ⁵³
19. ⁵Yaú ⁵löng ‚kán lok‚. Yat₂ yat₂ ⁵yaú ‚yan ‚kong-‚shü.	Have two [C.]. ³² Day (by) day have man preach.
20. Haí² ‚T‘ín-⁵Chü-káú² ke², pé² ‚Ye-‚sò-káú² ke² ‚ni? ²	Are Heaven's-Lord's-faith's, (or ¹⁵) or Jesus faith's, eh ? ¹⁵ ⁵³
21. Yat, ‚kán haí² ‚Ye-⁵sò káú² ke².	One [C.] is Jesus' faith's. ¹⁵
22. Yat, (or Ko²) ‚kán haí² ‚T‘ín ⁵Chü káú² ke².	One (or The other) [C.] is Heaven's Lord's faith's. ¹⁵
23. ‚Shan-fú² haí² ‚mi-‚yan• á² ?	Priests (Romish) are what-men, eh ? ²
24. Ko²-ko² ‚tò haí² Fát - ‚lán•-‚saí•-‚yan á².	Everyone even is Frenchman. ²
25. ⁵K‘öü-téí² ⁵yaú ká-kün ⁵mò ‚ni ? ²	They have families not, eh ? ⁵³
26. ‚M ⁵chun ⁵k‘öü ⁵ts'öü ⁵lò-‚p'o ke².	Not allowed to-them to-marry wives. ¹⁵
27. ⁵K‘öü pán² ‚T‘ong-‚chong ke² lok‚.	They dress Chinese-style. ¹⁵ ³²
28. ⁵Yaú mat, yí²-sz² ‚ni?²	Have what meaning, eh ? ⁵³
29. ⁵K‘öü ⁵söng hok₂ ‚fán ‚T‘ong-‚yan yat, yöng².	They wish copy again Chinese (lit. T'ong men, i.e., men of the T'ong Dynasty) one same.
30. Chung² ⁵yaú mat, yün-kwú² ⁵mò ‚ni ?²	Besides have what reason, have-not, eh ? ⁵³
31. Yíú² man² ⁵k‘öü tsaú² ‚chí lo².	Must ask them then know. ³¹
32. ⁵Ngo haí² ‚T‘óng-‚yan, ‚m ‚chí-tò² á. ²	I am Chinese, not know. ¹

LESSON XIII.—Nautical.

1.	This is a steamer.	呢隻係火船。
2.	That is a sailing vessel. [a steam-launch	嗰隻係桅槳船
3.	There is no wind to-day. We must go in	今日冇風、要搭火船仔去咯。
4.	How many passengers are there on board?	船上有幾多搭客呢
5.	Are there fully a thousand, or thereabout?	有成千個吤嘴冇呀
6.	They are mostly Chinese, who are going to Singapore.	唐人多咯、去星架波嘅
7.	Where is the Chief Officer? [Mate.	大伙呢、(or)大伙喺邊處吖
8.	This is the Captain; that is the Second	呢個係船主、嗰個係二伙
9.	When shall we reach port?	幾時到埠呀
10.	This vessel can go very fast.	呢隻船行得好快
11.	How many *li* will it go in an hour?	一點鐘行得幾多里路度呢
12.	It will probably steam over fifty *li*.	約嘆車得五十多里路
13.	Is it the Chief or Second Engineer who	係大車、嘆二車埋砦呢
14.	Do you ever sail? [has gone on shore?	有時哄哩冇呀
15.	How much coal do you use a day?	一日使幾多炭呢
16.	It depends entirely upon the speed of the	睇個隻船行快、嘆行慢嗻
17	If she goes fast then more is used; [ship.	車快就燒多、
18.	If she goes slow then less is used.	車慢就燒少
19.	Come up on deck. Do not go near the funnel.	上船面喇、咪行埋烟通個處呀
20.	Is this a passage boat, or a ferry-boat?	呢隻渡船、嘆橫水渡呢
21.	It is a passage boat; this is a Kau-lung passage boat.	係渡呀、呢隻係九龍渡呀、(頭)呢
22.	When do you start; and when do you arrive?	你幾時開身、 幾時到 [or埋
23.	Where is the ladies' cabin; and the pantry?	女艙呢、管事房呢
24.	Call the carpenter to mend that door.	叫鬪木佬嚟、整翻好個度門
25.	The hinges are off, and the lock is broken.	個的鉸用嘅、個鎖又爛
26.	It has no lock. The key has been lost.	冇鎖羅、唔見個條鎖匙咯
27.	Make another.	整過第二條喇
28.	First take a padlock, and lock the door securely.	先使把荷包鎖、鎖緊個度門至得
29.	How many sailors and firemen are there on board?	船上有幾多水手、幾多燒火呀
30.	What is the capacity of the vessel?	個船裝得幾多貨呢
31.	What is her draft? Seven feet eight.	食幾深水呀、 七尺八
32.	They are just going to hoist sail.	就扯哩羅

LESSON XIII.—Nautical.

1.	‿Ni chek₀ hai² ⸗fo-₍shün.	This [C.] is steamer.
2.	⸗Ko chek₀ hai² ₍wai-⸗p‛áng ₍shün.	That (C.) is sailing ship.
3.	₍Kam-yat₂ ⸗mò ₍fung. Yíú⸥ táp₀ ⸗fo-₍shün-⸗tsai hōü⸥ lok₀.	To-day no wind. Must by fire-ship-little go.³²
4.	₍Shün shöng² ⸗yaú ⸗kéí₀ to táp₀-hák₀ ₍ni?²	Ship on have how many passengers, eh?⁵³
5.	⸗Yaú ₍sheng† ₍ts‛ín ko⸥ kòm⸥ tsaí² ⸗mò ₀á?	Have fully thousand [C.] so thereabouts, not have?¹ eh?²
6.	₍T‛ong-₍yan ₍to lo⸥. Hōü⸥ ₍Sing-ká⸥-₀po ke⸥.	Chinese most.³¹ Going Singapore.¹⁵ [eh?¹
7.	Táí² ⸗fo ₍ni?² *or* Táí² ⸗fo ⸗haí pín shü⸥ ₀á?²	Chief mate, eh?⁵³ *or* Chief mate at what place,
8.	₍Ni-ko⸥ haí² ₍shün-⸗chü; ⸗ko-ko⸥ haí² yí²	This [C.] is Captain; that [C.] is second mate.
9.	⸗Kéí ₍shí• tò⸥ íaú² á⸥? [⸗fo.	What time arrive port, eh?²
10.	₍Ni chek₀ ₍shün ₍háng tak₂ ⸗hò fáí⸥.	This [C.] vessel go can very fast.
11.	Yat₂ ⸗tím ₍chung ₍háng tak₂ ⸗kéí ₀to ⸗léí lò² tò⸥•₀ ₍ni?² [lò².	One striking-of-the-clock go can how many miles road about, eh?⁵³
12.	Yŏk₋-mok₀• ₍ch‛e tak₂ ⸗ng-shap₂ ₍to ⸗léí	Probably steam can fifty more *li* road.
13.	Haí² Táí² ₍ch‛e, péí² yí² ₍ch‛e ₍máí cháí⸥	Is-it Chief engineer, or second do closed (to)
14.	⸗Yaú ₍shí• ⸗shaí ⸗léí ⸗mò á⸥? [₍ni?²	Have times use sails have-not, eh?² [shore, eh?⁵³
15.	Yat₂ yat₂ ⸗shaí ⸗kéí₀to t‛án⸥ ₍ni²?	One day use how much coal, eh?⁵³
16.	⸗T‛aí ko⸥ chek₀ ₍shün ₍háng fáí⸥, péí² ₍háng	See that [C.] vessel go fast, or go slow only.⁷
17.	₍Ch‛e fáí⸥ tsaú² ₍shíú₀to; [mán² ₍che.²	Steam fast then burn more;
18.	₍Ch‛e mán² tsaú² ₍shíú ⸗shíú.	Steam slow then burn little.
19.	⸗Shöng ₍shün mín⸗• ₍lá² ⸗Maí ₍háng ₍máí yín-₀t‛ung ko⸥ shü⸥ á⸥. [₍ni?²	Ascend ship's surface.²¹ Don't walk near funnel that place.²
20.	₍Ni chek₀ tò²-₍shün, péí² ₍wáng-⸗shŏü-tò⸗•	This [C.] passage-boat, or ferry-boat?⁵³
21.	Haí² tò⸥ á⸥; ₍ni chek₀ hai² ⸗Kaú-₍lung tò² á⸥ [₍máí ₍t‛aú) ₍ni?²	Is passage-boat;² this [C.] is Kau-lung passage-boat.² [connect-bows to-the-port), eh?⁵³
22.	⸗Néí ⸗kéí-₍shí• hoí-₍shan; ⸗kéí-₍shí• tò⸥ (or	You what-time start; what-time arrive (or
23.	⸗Nŏü ₍ts‛ong ₍ni?² ⸗Kwún-sz⸗•-₍fong• ₍ni?² [⸗ko tò² ₍mún.	Women's cabin, eh?⁵³ Pantry, eh?⁵³ [[C.] door.
24.	Kíú⸥ taú⸥-muk₂-₍lò ₍lai ⸗ching-₍fán-⸗hò	Call carpenter come, to-make-again-good that
25.	Ko⸥-₀ti káú⸥ lat₂⸗cho, ko⸥ ⸗so yaú⸥ lán². [lok₀.	Those hinges came-off [s. of p. t.], the lock moreover broken.
26.	⸗Mò ⸗so lo⸥. ₍M kín⸗• ko⸥ ₍t‛íú ⸗so-₍shí	No lock.³¹ Not see the [C.] lock-key.³²
27.	⸗Ching kwo² taí²-yí² ₍t‛íú ₍lá.	Make again another [C.].²¹
28.	Sín ⸗shaí ⸗pá ho-₀páú-⸗so, ⸗so ⸗kan ko⸥ tò² ₍mún chí⸥-tak₂.	First use [C.] purse-lock, lock firmly that [C.] door before it-will-do.
29.	₍Shün shöng² ⸗yaú ⸗kéí₀to ⸗shŏü-⸗shaú, ⸗kéí₀to ₍shíú-⸗fo á⸥?	Ship on have how many sailors (*lit.* water-hands), how many firemen (*lit.* burn-fire), eh?²
30.	Ko⸥ ₍shün ₍chong tak₂ ⸗kéí₀to fo⸥ ₍ni?²	That vessel hold can how many goods, eh?⁵³
31.	Shik₂ ⸗kéí ₍sham ⸗shŏü á⸥? Ts‛at₂ ch‛ek₀.	Eat how deep water, eh?² Seven feet eight.
32.	Tsaú² ⸗ch‛e ⸗léí lo⸥. [pát₀.	Just-about hauling-up sails³¹

LESSON XIV.—Judicial.

1.	I want to summons this man. [mine.	我想告呢個人.
2.	He is a thief, and has stolen things of	佢做賊、偷我野咯.
3.	Have you any witnesses ?	你有證人有叮.
4	I have witnesses ; they have not come yet.	有證人、唔曾嚟咯.
5.	Issue subpœnas for them to come.	出證人票、叫佢嚟喇.
6.	Has the constable arrived ?	差人 (*or* 差役 *or* 緑衣)¹ 到嗎.
7.	He is at the Gaol.	佢喺監房.
8.	This is the Yamen.	呢間衙門囉.
9	What Yamen ?	邊間衙門呢.
10.	The Consul's Yamen (Consulate).	領事官衙門囉.
11.	Who is the present Consul ?	而家邊個做領事官呢.
12.	Mr. Fut (*lit.* Mr. Buddha).	係佛大人呀.
13.	I will trouble you to present this petition for me to His Lordship, the Chief Justice	多煩你同我遞呢張稟過 按察司大人.
14.	Kindly tell me what to say.	唔該你教我點講.
15.	Are you Plaintiff, or Defendant ?	你係原告、嚊被告呢.
16.	You must tell the truth, and only say what you have seen and heard yourself.	要照直講、親眼見. 親耳聽、至好講出嚟.
17.	Then I must just say what I know myself.	噉我硬要講本身所知嘅事咯.
18	That is right; that is quite right; no mistake.	啱咯、啱嗤咯、冇錯咯.
19.	Your evidence is not believed.	你口供唔入信呀.
20.	The evidence given on both sides does not agree.	兩頭口供唔合叮.
21.	One of you must be telling lies	是但有個講大話咯.
22.	No, I am not. All Hongkong knows about this matter.	唔係、冇講大話、通香港都 知呢件事咯.
23	If you had said, ' the whole neighbourhood also knows,' I might perhaps have believed you.	你話通街坊都知、我或者 可以信你.
24.	Will His Lordship allow us to go to the temple and swear on a cock's head ?	大人准我哋去廟斬鷄頭 唔准呢.
25.	How many prisoners are there to-day ?	今日有幾多犯呢.
26.	There is a murderer, there are five thieves, two burglars, and three kidnappers.	有個兇手、五個賊、兩個打明 火嘅、三個拐帶嘅.

1. 差人 ₍ch'ái ₍yan, and 差役 ₍ch'ái yik₂ are better than 緑衣 luk₂ ₍yi which is vulgar.

LESSON XIV.—Judicial.

1.	⊂Ngo ⸀sŏng kò⸃ ₍ni ko⸃ ₍yan.	I wish prosecute this [C.] man
2.	⸀K'öü tsò² ts'ák₎, ₍t'aú ⸂ngo ⸀ye lok₀	He does thief, (as a calling), steal my things. [32]
3.	⸀Néí ⸀yaú ching⸃-₍yan ⸂mò ₍á?²	You have witness not-have, eh? [1]
4.	⸀Yaú ching⸃-₍yan; ₍m-₍ts'ang ₍laí lok₀	Have witness; not yet come. [32]
5.	Ch'ut₎ ching⸃-₍yan-p'íú⸃ kíú⸃ ⸀k'öü ₍laí lá.²	Issue subpœnas call them come. [21]
6.	₍Ch'áí ₍yan (or ₍ch'áí yik₎, or luk₂ ₀yí) tò⸃ ⸂má?	Police man (or police man, or green clothes) arrived, eh? [37]
7.	⸀K'öü ⸂haí ₍kám-₍fong.	He at Gaol.
8.	₍Ni ₍kán ₍ngá-₍mún* lo⸃.	This [C.] Yamen. [31]
9.	Pín ₍kán ₍ngá-₍mún* (or ₍mún) ₍ni? ²	Which [C.] Yamen, eh? [53]
10.	⸀Ling-sz²-₍kwún ₍ngá-₍mún lo⸃.	Consul's Yamen. [31]
11.	₍Yí-₍ká ₀pín ko⸃ tsò² ⸀Ling-sz²-₍kwún ₍ni? ²	At-present who [C.] is-doing consul, eh? [53]
12.	Haí² Fat₎ Táí²-₍Yan á⸃.	It-is Fat Great-man (i.e., Mr. Buddha).²
13.	₍To ₍fán ⸂néí ₍t'ung ⸀ngo taí² ₍ni ₍chöng ⸂pan kwo⸃ On⸃-Ch'át₋₀Sz Táí²-₍Yan.	Much trouble you for me present this [C.] petition to Chief-Justice His-Lordship.
14.	₍M ₍koí ⸀néí káú⸃ ⸀ngo ⸂tím ⸂kong.	Not deserve you teach me how speak.
15.	⸀Néí haí² ₍Yün-kò⸃, pé² Péí²-kò⸃ ₍ni? ²	You are Plaintiff, or Defendant, eh? [53]
16.	Yíú⸃ chíú⸃ chik₎ ⸂kong₀ ts'an ⸂ngán kin⸃, ts'an ⸂yí ₍t'engt₊ chí⸃ ⸂hò ⸂kong ch'ut₎ ₍laí.	Must according-to straight-forwardness speak, own eyes seen, own ears heard, only good speak out come.
17.	⸂Kòm ⸂ngo ngáng² yíú⸃ ⸂kong ⸂pún ₍shan ⸂sho ₍chí ke⸃ sz² lok₀	Then I just must speak own person what (I) know [15] matters. [32]
18.	₍Ngám (or ₍ngám) lok₀; ₍ngám (or ₍ngám) saí⸃ lok₀; ⸂mò t'so⸃ lok₀	Right; [32] right entirely; [32] no mistake. [32]
19.	⸀Néí ⸂haú-₍kung ₍m yap₂ sun⸃ á⸃.	Your evidence not enter belief.²
20.	⸀Lŏng ₍t'aú ⸂haú-₍kung ₍m kòp₀ á.²	Both sides evidence not agree.₁ [lies.³²]
21.	Shí²-tán² ⸀yaú* ko⸃ ⸂kong táí²-wá² lok₀	Certainly (of the two) there-is [C.] speaking
22.	₍M haí², ⸀mò ⸂kong táí²-wá². ₍T'ung ₍Hŏng-⸂Kong ₀tò ₍chí ₍ni kín² sz² lok₀	Not is, not speaking great-words. Throughout Hongkong (all) even know this [C.] matter. [32]
23.	⸀Néí wá², ᛫ ₍T'ung ₍káí-₍fong ₀tò ₍chí,' ⸀ngo wák₎-⸂che ⸂ho-₍yí sun⸃ ⸂néí.	You say, 'all neighbourhood even knows,' I perhaps might believe you.
24.	Táí²-₍Yan ⸂chun ⸀ngo-téí⸃ höü⸃ míú⁵* ⸂chám ₍kaí ₍t'aú, ₍m ⸂chun₀ ₍ni? ²	His-Lordship allow us go temple chop-off fowl's head, not allow, eh? [53]
25.	₍Kam-mat₎ ⸀yaú ⸂kéí ₀to fán⁵* ₍ni? ²	This-day have how many prisoners, eh? [53]
26.	⸀Yaú ko⸃ hung-⸂shaú, ⸀ng ko⸃ ts'ák₎, ⸀lŏng ko⸃ ⸂tá-₍ming-⸂fo ke⸃, ₍sám ko⸃ ⸂kwáí-táí⸃ ke⸃.	Have [C.] murderer, five [C.] thieves, two [C.] burglars, [15] three [C.] kidnappers. [15]

LESSON XIV.—Judicial.—*(Continued)*.

27. Then there are a great number of cases. 嗷、有好多案件咯。
28. Those are the lawyers at the table. 坐埋檯嘅係狀師咯。
29. The case has been up for hearing several times; when will judgment be given? 審幾堂羅、幾時定案呢。
30. How do I know? Ask the Interpreter to enquire for you. 我點知呀、　拜託傳話同你問吓喇。
31. The case was tried at the Magistracy, and the Magistrate allowed the defendant to be bailed out. 喺巡理廳審過、大老爺准担保被告出嚟咯。
32. Do you wish to arrest the man, or put execution in force against his goods? 你想拉個人、或 *(or* 嘵*)* 封佢貨呢。

LESSON XV.—Educational.

1. Ah! here we are. This is a Government Free School [classes. 啊、到咯、呢間係皇家義學。
2. There are sixty scholars, divided into four 有六十個學生、分四班嘅、
3. The master is a friend of mine, and a Chinese B.A. 個先生係我朋友、佢係秀才。
4. Has he got any assistant? 有人帮教冇呢。
5. Not at present, but he wishes to engage one after the New Year. 現時冇、但係過年想請個、
6. There will be holidays at the end of the year, I suppose? 年尾放假羅唄。
7. Certainly, we Chinese think it of the utmost importance to keep the New Year. 定嘅喇、我哋唐人過年算至緊要嘅咯。
8. What book is this boy reading? 呢個呢、讀乜野書呢。
9. That is the Trimetrical Classic, the book that a Chinese boy reads first. 個部係三字經咯、唐人細佬仔先讀個部嘅咯。
10. Then it is a simple book; for probably you proceed from the simple to the difficult. 嗷就係淺書咯、大概自淺而深嚟學嘅。
11. It is neither very simple, nor very difficult: the words are most of them simple, but the meaning is sometimes very abstruse. 又唔係幾淺、又唔係幾深、字大多淺嘅、但意思有時好深嘅。
12. How many years have you been at school? 你讀幾多年書呢。

LESSON XIV.—Judicial.—*(Continued)*.

27. ⟨Kòm, ⟨yaú ⟨hò ⟨to on⟩-kín⟩• lok⟨.   Then have great many cases.³²

28. ⟨T'so ⟨máí ⟨t'oí• ke⟩ haí² chong²-⟨sz lok⟨.   Sit at table those are lawyers.³²

29. ⟨Sham ⟨kéi ⟨t'ong lo⟩; ⟨kéi ⟨shí• ting² on⟩ ⟨ni?²   Try several sittings;³¹ what time fix case eh?⁵³

30. ⟨Ngo ⟨tim ⟨chi á⟩? Páí⟩-t'ok⟨ ⟨ch'ün-wá⟩• ⟨t'ung ⟨néi man² ⟨há ⟨lá.¹²   I how know, eh?² Beg-on-your-behalf Interpreter for you ask a-bit.²¹

31. ⟨Hai ⟨Ts'un-⟨léi-⟨t'eng (*or* ⟨t'eng) ⟨sham kwo⟩, Táí²-⟨lò-⟨ye ⟨chun ⟨tám-⟨pò Péí²-kò⟩ ch'ut⟨ ⟨laí lok⟨.   At Magistracy tried over, His-Worship allowed bail Defendant out come.³²

32. ⟨Néi ⟨sŏng ⟨láí ko⟩ ⟨yan, wák⟨ (*or* pé²) ⟨fung ⟨k'öü fo⟩ ⟨ni?²   You wish arrest the man, or seize his goods, eh?⁵³

LESSON XV.—Educational.

1. O²! tò⟩ lo⟩. ⟨Ni ⟨kán hai² ⟨Wong-⟨ká yí² hok⟨.•   Ah! Arrived.³¹ This [C.] is Government Free Study.

2. ⟨Yaú luk₂-shap₂ ko⟩ hok₂-⟨shángt (*or short* a), ⟨fan sz⟩ ⟨pán ke⟩.   Have sixty [C.] scholars, divided-into four classes.¹⁵

3. Ko⟩ ⟨Sín-⟨Shángt haí² ⟨ngo ⟨p'ang-⟨yaú; ⟨k'öü hai² Saú⟩-⟨ts'oí.•   The teacher is my friend; he is B.A.

4. ⟨Yaú ⟨yan ⟨pong-káú⟩ ⟨mò ⟨ni?²   Have man assist-teach not, eh?⁵³

5. Yín²-⟨shi ⟨mò, tán²-hai² kwo⟩• ⟨nín ⟨sŏng ⟨ts'eng ko⟩.   At-present no, but over (New) Year wishes engage [C.].

6. ⟨Nin ⟨méí fong⟩-ká⟩ lo⟩-kwá⟩?   Year end holidays³¹ probably?¹⁷

7. Ting⟩•-ke⟩ ⟨lá,² ⟨ngo-téí² ⟨T'ong-⟨yan kwo⟩ ⟨nín sün⟩ chí⟩ ⟨kan-yíú⟩ ke⟩-lok⟨.   Certainly,¹⁵ ²¹ we Chinese passing (New)-year consider most important.¹⁵ ³²

8. ⟨Ni-ko⟩ ⟨ni, tuk₂ mat₂-⟨ye ⟨shü ⟨ni?²   This [C.] now, reads what book eh?⁵³

9. Ko⟩ pò² hai² ⟨Sám-Tsz²-⟨king lo⟩. ⟨T'ong-⟨yan saí⟩-⟨man-⟨tsaí ⟨sín tuk₂ ko⟩ pò² ke⟩ lok⟨.   That [C.] is Three-Character-Classic.³¹ Chinese children first read that [C.]¹⁵ ³²

10. ⟨Kòm tsaú² haí² ⟨ts'ín ⟨shü lok⟨. Táí²-⟨k'oí tsz² ⟨ts'ín ⟨yí ⟨sham ⟨laí hok₂ ke⟩.   Then just is easy book.³² Probably from simple to difficult come study.¹⁵

11. Yaú² ⟨m haí² ⟨kéi ⟨ts'ín, yaú² ⟨m haí² ⟨kéi ⟨sham. Tsz² táí² ⟨to ⟨ts'ín ke⟩, tán² yí⟩-sz⟩ ⟨yaú-⟨shí ⟨hò ⟨sham ke⟩.   Also not is very shallow, also not is very deep. Characters greater many shallow,¹⁵ but sense have times very deep.¹⁵

12. ⟨Néi tuk₂ ⟨kéi ⟨to ⟨nin ⟨shü ⟨ni?²   You read how many years books, eh?⁵³

LESSON XV.—Educational.—(Continued).

13.	I have studied between ten and twenty years.	我讀十幾年書咯.
14.	Then you must be very learned.	噉你就係好有學問嘅咯.
15.	Oh no! I cannot consider myself as very learned.	唔係、我唔敢話自已好有學問嘅.
16.	Where is your desk ; where is your seat ?	你個書位(*or* 書檯, *or* 檯)呢、你嘅椅呢.
17.	I do not belong to this school, I have only come to visit—to see the teacher	我唔係做學生吖 我不過嚟坐吓哋、嚟見吓個教館先生啫.
18.	Oh! probably you are a student. Have you passed any examinations yet ?	啊、你係讀書人嘅 考過試咁曾呢.
19.	I have gone up several times, but have not graduated : my brother has taken his M.A.	考過兩三勻、未曾入、我大佬已經中舉咯.
20.	When does this class say its lessons ?	呢班幾時念書呢.
21.	We Chinese don't do that way ; when a boy knows his lesson he comes up and repeats it, the whole class does not come up at once.	我地唐人唔係噉嘅、一個讀熟、就一個嚟背、唔係成班一齊上嚟念嘅.
22.	If he does not know it, what then ?	或唔識呢、點呢.
23.	He has to go back to his place and learn it well, if he is lazy he is beaten.	要翻去位讀熟咯、若係懶惰就打佢咯.
24.	These are reading the Four Books, and those the Five Classics.	呢啲讀四書、嗰啲讀五經.
25.	It would be well to hang up two more maps in this school of yours.	你呢間書館 掛多兩幅地理圖都好吖.
26.	How many have commenced to write essays ?	有幾多個開筆作文章嘅呢.
27.	A number of the scholars can construct antithetical sentences I suppose.	有好多學生噲對對嘅.
28.	Bring ink, penholder, and pen nibs. I have brought them.	摔墨水、筆竿、筆嘴嚟喇、拈嚟咯.
29.	Has the Government Inspector of Schools been to see this school ?	皇家書館嘅監督有嚟踱過呢間館冇呢.
30.	He has ; he has been several times. He comes every now and then.	有、嚟過好幾勻咯、耐不耐都嚟嘅.
31.	How many names are there on the roll ?	日記紙有幾多人名呢.
32.	There are sixty odd ; two or three are absent on sick leave.	有六十幾個、有兩三個因有病告假.

LESSON XV.—Educational.—*(Continued)*.

13. ꜱNgo tuk₂ shap₂ ꜛkéi ꜀nín ꜀shü lok.

I read ten odd years books. [32]

14. ꜛKòm ꜱnéi tsaú² hai² ꜛhò ꜱyaú hok₂-man² ke² lok

Then you even are very-much possessed of learning. [15] [32]

15. ꜀M hai², ꜱngo ꜀m ꜛkòm wá² tsz²-ꜛkéi ꜛhò ꜱyaú hok₂-man² ke².

Not am, I not dare say myself very-much possessed-of learning. [15]

16. ꜱNéi ko² shü-waí⁵• (*or* shü-꜀t'oí*, *or* ꜀to'í*) ni; ꜱnéi-ke² ꜛyí ꜀ni? [2]

Your [*C.*] desk (*or* table), eh; [53] your seat, eh? [53]

17. ꜱNgo ꜀m hai²-tsò² hok₂-꜀shángꜞ (*or short* a) ꜀á, ꜱngo pat₂-kwo² ꜀laí ꜱts'o ꜱhá ꜀che, ꜀laí kín² ꜱhá ko² káú²-ꜛkwún ꜀Sín-Sháng (*or* ꜀Sengꜞ) ꜀che.

I not am school-boy, [1] I only come sit a-little while only, [7] come see a-bit that teach-school gentleman (*or contracted form*) only. [8]

18. O²! ꜱnéi haí² tuk₂-꜀shü-꜀yan kwá². ꜛHáú kwo² shí² ꜀m-꜀ts'ang ꜀ni? [2]

Oh! you are read-book-man probably. [18] Examined passed not-yet, eh? [53]

19. ꜛHáú kwo² ꜱlŏng ꜀sám ꜀wan, méí²-꜀ts'ang yap₂; ꜱngo táí²-ꜛlò ꜱyí-꜀king chung³• ꜛköü lok.

Examinations over two three times, not yet entered; my elder-brother already passed M.A. [32]

20. ꜀Ni ꜀pan ꜛkéi-꜀shí• ním²-꜀shü ꜀ni? [2]

This class what-time say-lesson, eh? [53]

21. ꜱNgo-téi² ꜀T'ong-꜀yan ꜀m haí² ꜛkòm ke², yat₂ ko² tuk₂-shuk₂, tsaú² yat₂ ko² ꜀laí púí², ꜀m haí² ꜀shengꜞ ꜀pán yat₂ ꜀ts'aí• ꜱshöng ꜀laí ním² ke².

We Chinese not are so, [15] one [*C.*] learned-thoroughly then one [*C.*] comes back-it, (*i. e., says his lesson with his back to the teacher: so that he cannot see the book the teacher holds*) not is whole class one to-gether up come say. [15]

22. Wák₂ ꜀m shik ꜀ni, ꜛtím ꜀ni? [2]

If not know, eh, how then? [53]

23. Yíú² ꜀fán höü² waí⁵• tuk₂ shuk₂ lok, yŏk₂ hai² ꜱlán-to² tsaú² ꜛtá ꜱk'öü lok.

Must back go seat read thoroughly, [32] if is lazy then beat him. [32]

24. ꜀Ni-꜀ti tuk₂ Sz²-꜀Shü; ꜛko-꜀ti tuk₂ ꜱNg-King.

These learning Four Books; those learning Five Classics.

25. ꜱNéi ꜀ni ꜀kán shü-ꜛkwun kwá² ꜀to ꜱlŏng fuk₂ téi² ꜱléí-꜀t'ò ꜀tò ꜛhò ꜀á. [2]

You this [*C.*] school hang more two [*C*] maps also good. [1]

26. ꜱYaú ꜛkéi ꜀to ko² ꜀hoí pat₂ tsok₂ ꜀man-꜀chöng ke² ꜀ni? [2]

Have how many [*C.*] start (with) pens compose essays, [15] eh? [53]

27. ꜱYaú ꜛhò ꜀to hok₂-꜀shángꜞ (*or short* a) ꜱwúí töü² töü³• kwá².

Have great many scholars can make antitheses, I-suppose. [18]

28. ꜀Ning mak₂-ꜛshöü, pat₂-꜀kon, pat₂-ꜛtsöü ꜀laí ꜀lá. [2] ꜀Ním ꜀laí• lok.

Bring ink, pen-holder, pen-nib come. [21] Brought come. [32]

29. ꜱWong-꜀Ká ꜀shü-ꜛkwún-ke² ꜀Kám-tuk₂, ꜱyaú ꜀laí ꜛt'aí kwo² ꜀ni ꜀kán ꜛkwún ꜱmó ꜀ni? [2]

Government Schools' Inspector have come look over this [*C.*] school, not, eh? [53]

30. ꜱYaú, ꜀laí kwo² ꜛhò ꜛkéi ꜀wan lok, noí²-pat₂-noí⁵• ꜀tò ꜀laí ke². [꜀ni? [2]

Have come over good few times, [32] now-and-then also come. [15]

31. Yat₂-kéí²-ꜛchi ꜱyau ꜛkéi ꜀to ꜀yan ꜀meng•

Roll have how many persons' names, eh? [53]

32. ꜱYaú luk₂-shap₂ ꜛkéi ko²; ꜱyaú ꜱlŏng ꜀sám ko² ꜀yan ꜱyaú peng²ꜞ kò² ká².

Have sixty odd [*C.*]. Have two three [*C.*] be-cause have sickness report leave.